BARUCH'S

An Ethiopian Jew's Struggle to Save His People

ODYSSEY

BARUCH TEGEGNE

as told to Phyllis Schwartzman Pinchuk

gefen publishing house

JERUSALEM ♦ NEW YORK

Typesetting: Jerusalem Typesetting
Cover Design: S. Kim Glassman

ISBN 978-965-229-404-3

1 3 5 7 9 8 6 4 2

Gefen Publishing House, Ltd.   Gefen Books
6 Hatzvi Street, Jerusalem 94386, Israel   600 Broadway, Lynbrook, NY 11563, USA
972-2-538-0247   516-593-1234
orders@gefenpublishing.com   orders@gefenpublishing.com

www.israelbooks.com

Printed in Israel   Send for our free catalogue

Contents

SECTION 2 WANDERING JEW

SECTION 3 THE PROMISED LAND

Introduction

N obody knows exactly how or when the Jews arrived and settled in Ethiopia, a land known as Cush in the Bible. Some scholars believe that they had settled there some three thousand years ago, during the reign of King Solomon and the Cushite Queen of Sheba. Others suggest that survivors of the tribes of Dan, Naphtali, and Gad fled to Egypt after the Babylonians destroyed the kingdom of Judah and the First Temple in 586 BCE, then followed the Blue Nile to northern Ethiopia, where they made their homes on its fertile soil. Still others advance the theory that we are descendants of refugees who ran away from Roman persecution after the destruction of the Second Temple in 70 CE. Although our origins are somewhat obscure, the latter course of our history is undisputed:

By the tenth century CE a flourishing autonomous Falasha kingdom encompassed as many as one million people. For several centuries, this Jewish kingdom held its own against Christian and Muslim antagonists. But by the early seventeenth century, the Falashas were overwhelmed, and their land confiscated. Many were sold into slavery, and the remainder were forced to convert to Christianity. Only after years of poverty and suffering were the remnants of the once-proud Jewish kingdom permitted to resume practicing their religion.

No longer permitted to own land, the Falashas leased small farms or worked in crafts. Most settled in Ethiopia's mountainous northwest Gondar region and scattered throughout 400 small villages.*

The Scottish anthropologist James Bruce, while researching the course of the Blue Nile in 1770, was surprised to come across a whole community of black Jews in the mountains where the great river originated. He published his astonishing discovery in a London paper. Years later, from 1860 to 1904, members of the London Society for the Conversion of the Jews set out to this remote territory, determined to "save the souls" of these forsaken people. The Jews, however, fled further and further into the hills in order to avoid them. Nevertheless, the society succeeded in converting thousands of my people to Christianity.

In 1864, the eminent Orthodox leader Rabbi Azriel Hildesheimer issued a call from Berlin to the European Jewish community for action against the intrusions of the Christian missionaries. He sent a message to the Falashas saying, "Don't lose faith, my brothers. Have confidence! Never yet have the unfortunate knocked on the door of a Jewish house without having found assistance. You are our brothers; you are our own flesh and blood!"

In 1867, the Alliance Israélite Universelle of France, funded by Baron Edmond de Rothschild, sent Joseph Halevy, the renowned professor of Semitic languages at the Sorbonne, to investigate. When he arrived at a Jewish village in Ethiopia, nobody believed he was Jewish. Everyone thought he was a Christian missionary. Since Ethiopian Christians did not eat meat slaughtered by Jews, his hosts, out of hospitality, brought him an animal to slaughter by

---

* Diane Winston, "The Falashas: History and Analysis of Policy towards a Beleaguered Community," *Perspectives* (New York: National Jewish Resource Center, April 1980).

himself according to his own custom. But he said, "No, I'm a Jew from Jerusalem." Word went out from village to village that there was a Jewish visitor from Jerusalem and before long the leaders from each village gathered to hear what he had to say. They asked him many questions: How many Jews are there in Jerusalem? Are they free to practice their religion? Is there a new Temple in Jerusalem? Which holy places still exist? Are there places like Bet Lechem, Har Hagrizim, Nazareth, and Har Tabor? (All these namesakes appear in Ethiopia.)

Joseph Halevy answered their questions one by one and proceeded to inform them that there were Jews all over the world. They couldn't believe it. For hundreds of years they had thought they were the only Jews left on earth. After more lively exchanges, Halevy learned that these Jews faithfully practiced all the rituals prescribed in the Bible – but most of their practices ended with the laws in the Bible. Although their scholars had memorized much of the Oral Law, the community's connection with the rest of the Jewish world was cut off before the great books of biblical interpretations were written. They knew nothing about the Mishnah, Gemara or Talmud, where the Oral Law was codified for posterity, nor were they aware of any of the later Rabbinic writings, such as those of Rashi or Maimonides. They had retained some of the ancient writings, like the Book of the Maccabees, which were not included in the Tanach ("Old Testament"), and celebrated Hanukkah – the dedication of the Second Temple, thanks to the Maccabees – differently from how it is done today.

Their dietary laws were somewhat different, too. For example, kosher animals (which have cleft hooves and chew their cud) were slaughtered according to the rigorous methods prescribed in the Bible. But they differed from Rabbinic Judaism in their interpretation of the commandment in Deuteronomy 14:21 which states: "Thou shalt not seethe a kid in its mother's milk." The rabbis had interpreted this to mean that meat and milk products may not be mixed together. Consequently, many laws evolved elaborating this precept, including waiting a prescribed amount of time between eating meat and dairy foods and keeping separate sets of dishes and utensils for each food group – one set for meat and one for dairy. Ethiopian Jews, however, took this to mean that you mustn't cook a baby animal while it is still nursing – in other words, until it is at least one year old.

Our religious scholars and leaders or priests are called *kohanim* (from Hebrew) or *kessim*. We never did have rabbis. Our *kessim* developed our own interpretive books of the Bible. Halevy's student, Jacob (Jacques) Faitlovitch, who came to Ethiopia in 1904, spent two and a half years translating these books from the ancient Ethiopian language Ge'ez into Hebrew. He also researched and documented our history and culture.

Upon returning to Europe, Faitlovich organized a Pro-Falasha Committee in Italy. Soon after that, the first Pro-Falasha Committee was created in the USA. Faitlovitch, with the help of these organizations, and with the cooperation of the Jewish community in Egypt, opened a school in Ethiopia to give the Jews the knowledge and strength required to protect themselves against persecution and from the persistent Christian missionaries.

The Ethiopian Jews were called Falashas by the rest of the population, which means "outsiders," as we were generally not allowed to own land and were not part of the mainstream culture. We, however, prefer to call ourselves "Bet Yisrael" (House of Israel, sometimes spelled "Beta Yisrael").

Experience taught us that the Christian Ethiopians had ambivalent feelings towards the Jews. Sometimes they showed us great respect, because the royal family claimed to be descendants of King Solomon and the Queen of Sheba. For example, Haile Selassie (1892–1975), emperor of Ethiopia (1930–36; 1941–74), bore with great pride the title of "Lion of Judah." But mostly it was the peasants who feared the Jews. They were suspicious of our "strange" religion and believed that during the night the Jews turned into hyenas, who kidnapped and ate their children! Such preposterous lies and superstitions poisoned their minds.

After Faitlovitch had managed to educate a group of Bet Yisrael students, he sent twenty-five of them to *yeshivot* (Jewish schools) – ten to Israel and fifteen to different European countries – to study modern Judaism. Most of these students went back to Ethiopia to teach others what they had learned.

When Faitlovitch died in 1955, his home in Tel Aviv, including his vast library, was bequeathed to the Ethiopian Jews in Israel. Unfortunately, after the municipality took possession, all his books were distributed to various libraries, making it very difficult to do research on Ethiopia in one central place. Sad to say, even his home was allowed to deteriorate.

SECTION 1

From the Home of My Father

Chapter 1

G randfather Tegegne Tamno gazed at me intently, hesitated for a moment, then held me up high and proclaimed to the assembled men: "Henceforth he shall be known as Baruch (Blessed) Tegegne, for I have found blessing in him." I then continued my whimpering even more vehemently, since I had just been the subject of a *brit milah*, the ritual circumcision of a Hebrew male child, performed eight days after birth.

This happened in 1944 in a remote Ethiopian hillside village of about two hundred families, called Wozaba, one of the nearly five hundred Jewish villages scattered in the hills of Ethiopia. The families lived in *tikul*s, or mud huts, covered with pointed grass roofs. The fifty-odd *tikul*s in Wozaba were built in a circle around the synagogue, which had two sections, one for the women and one for the men, and a *Magen David* (Star of David) standing proudly on its roof. Each circular hut had a dividing wall that separated the kitchen from the living quarters. There was no such thing as indoor plumbing; we used the bushes or an outside hut that had a hole dug in the center. Our bathtub was the river. For soap, we used what we called *indod*, aromatic dried seeds that lathered up when rubbed in water. We lived close to a Christian village, but had little contact with its inhabitants.

When I was an infant, my parents were obliged to go – by

foot – to a funeral quite far away. As Mother was pregnant again, they feared it would be too difficult to carry me all the way, so they placed me in the charge of my maternal grandparents. When my parents returned and tried to take me home, I clung to Grandfather so tightly, they couldn't pry me away. "Leave him!" Grandfather ordered. And so they did. That's how I came to be raised by my adoring and adored grandfather. I felt so close to him that I used to call him "Abba" (meaning "father" both in Hebrew and Amharic).

Grandfather was a special man. He was tall and thin, with a long Semitic face that sported an impressive beard. He was very religious and every year he was prepared, as were other of his kinsmen, to take the long walk to Jerusalem. He even tried it once. He and some friends had set out along the Wozaba valley, up to Massawa, and along the Red Sea, but they never did make it to the Holy Land. Now they were waiting for the Messiah to lead them there. "Abba" was very wise. He taught me that in order to see properly you have to use not only your eyes, but your conscience as well. I have never forgotten these words. He was respected by everyone in the whole area, Jew and Gentile alike, and was often asked to settle all kinds of disputes, between Jew and Jew, Jew and Christian, and Christian and Christian. His mother lived with us and amazingly lived to the ripe old age of one hundred twelve. (She even outlived my grandfather.)

"Abba" was one of the few Jews allowed to farm as much land as he wished. Most Jews couldn't possess land, because almost all the arable land was held by hereditary tenure of generations of Ethiopians. And so, nearly all the men were restricted to doing metal work, such as fashioning axes, knives, farm implements, scissors, guns, and the like; making leather goods, like saddles and reins; or weaving tapestries. Some were hired by the landowners to cultivate their land. They worked very hard, for it was often rocky and overgrown with bushes. Their wives or children would bring their lunches in the sun-baked fields. Though considered a man of wealth by his community, "Abba" never gave up hope of going to Jerusalem. That was his dream.

Grandmother was a very quiet woman, who toiled from sunrise to sunset and never complained. I used to call her "*Inat*," which means "Mother" in Amharic. She would tell me stories about her mother's side of the family. They were staunch defenders of the Jews. Once, while her uncle, Adigche Aymlak, was swimming in the river, a group of seven Christians came along and tried to kill him. Miraculously he fought them off, except for one, who attacked him with a knife. He slashed my great uncle's hand and cut off one of his fingers. He remained partially incapacitated for the rest of his life.

An ancestral grandmother, on grandmother's side, renowned for creating exceptionally beautiful pottery, had once presented the king with an exquisite piece of her work. He was so impressed by her craftsmanship and artistry that he absolved her family from paying taxes for many generations to come.

The women in our villages, aside from cooking meals and raising children, produced wonderful ceramics, as did their ancestors. They used to go down to the Gondar City market to sell their products, but the potential buyers, knowing how difficult it was for them to carry the unsold pottery back up the hill, would wait until the end of the day to buy the remaining stock at very low prices. This bothered my grandfather very much. Besides, he worried that the Christians would try to convert these innocent women and girls while on their territory. To avert these problems, he decided to set up booths along the highway close to our village for them to sell their wares. This venture turned out to be very successful.

"Abba" had attended Faitlovitch's school and was so impressed by what he had learned that he built a school for Jewish boys in our community with the help of all the people in the village. Mother became the cook in an adjacent building. Even today I have fond memories of the wonderful Shabbat bread (*dabo*) she used to bake, which looked like a big pita; and the thought of her delicious meat sauce (*wat*) still makes my mouth water.

As to my paternal family, my father told me that Christians had killed his father because he had made the fatal mistake of allowing his mule to graze on the landowner's land. Father avenged this murder by killing the brutal Christian. Consequently father's family was in continuous danger, because now the Christian's family members were out to take revenge on his loved ones. Upon hearing that they were on his trail, Father knew he had to do something drastic to save his family. So he divorced his first wife, changed his name to avoid discovery, then took his surviving son and fled with him to the village of Wozaba. There he met my beautiful mother, married her, and they proceeded to have seven children – three girls and four boys. I was third in line. When after fifteen years, news of the approaching enemy reached him once again, he divorced my mother, went off to a different village, remarried, and fathered an additional three children. All his life he lived in perpetual fear that his enemies would come after his beloved children and cause a catastrophe.

Baruch's mother, in Ethiopia

Baruch's father, 1992

Chapter II

I was a very happy child and always looked forward with great anticipation to our religious festivals. As we lived apart from the Christians, we observed our particular holidays in our own traditional ways. My favorite of them all was Rosh Hashanah, the New Year celebration. Our Ethiopian calendar was similar to the Jewish lunar/solar *luach* (calendar), but slightly different. We had twelve lunar months of thirty days each, with five days remaining to make up for the solar year of three hundred sixty-five days. Those five days were spent in purification rites, going to the *mikvah* (ritual bath) and praying for forgiveness for our sins. We children would gather wild yellow flowers from the fields and go in groups from house to house presenting bouquets to the ladies, while wishing them a "Happy New Year." They, in return, gave us small gifts. It was a beautiful, memorable experience.

Yom Kippur (the Day of Atonement) was an austere day of fasting. This was the culmination of ten days of penitence beginning with the first day of Rosh Hashanah. People were careful to be pure and clean while asking for forgiveness. Often during the praying and singing, they would jump up at intervals to make themselves physically weak and humble before God.

Succot (the Feast of Booths), which follows four days after Yom Kippur, is a reminder of the Jewish people's sojourn in the desert after the Exodus and also a time to give thanks for the harvest. Thanksgiving was celebrated twice among our people – once on Succot and again when our own harvest was collected, sometimes in January. We called that holiday B'ala Matsalat.

On the day before the holiday of Purim, at the end of the Fast of Esther, the community ate and drank together and then our *kes* read aloud *Megillat Esther* (the biblical Book of Esther). Purim had none of the trappings connected with it today; there were no masquerades, carnivals, merrymaking, or drinking. It was a more solemn occasion.

Pesach (Passover) was very serious. We were strictly forbidden to have any *chametz* (leavened dough) in the house. A week before the holiday, houses were cleaned from top to bottom. Women washed everything; if you glanced near the river, you'd see the whole mountain covered with linens and clothes drying in the sun. Those who could afford it bought new clothing. We children gathered reeds from the river to place in our homes to remind us of the crossing of the *Yam Suf* (Sea of Reeds) and the joyous song sung by Miriam (Moses' sister) upon arriving safely on the other shore with her people – the Jewish slaves who had escaped from the Egyptians. We used to honor our elders by bringing them a straight sapling with a forked tip, which we called *batra Mose* (staff of Moses). I did this for my "Abba" many times.

During the day, before the first night of Pesach, the community's *shohet* (ritual slaughterer) went from house to house and slaughtered whatever animal the family could afford to give him, e.g., a lamb, a chicken, etc. Before sundown, each household brought its own freshly roasted offering, which the *kohen* blessed, and then divided among the whole congregation so that we could all have our Seder (ritual meal) together. Round, flat *matzot* were baked for the whole community in the synagogue that day. After we all sat down, the *kes* would relate the story of Moses and everyone – even the children – listened with rapt attention. I found out later that the story he used to tell us – which had been handed down through the ages – had more details in it than are included in the modern Haggadah. For seven days we ate no *chametz* and at the end of the holiday a lamb or a goat was slaughtered for another festive communal feast.

We celebrated Shavuot (the Feast of Weeks), the Giving of the Torah, as do the people of Israel today. Nowadays, my people in Israel make it a point to walk to Jerusalem as our ancestors did in Temple times.

We had our own unique holiday, called Sigd. Once a year all the Jewish villagers got together in Ambover to pray for our return to Israel. Everyone fasted beforehand. "Abba" used to take me there, but he instructed me to eat, since I was not obliged to fast until I was thirteen years old – the age of bar mitzvah – when I became responsible for my own actions. (By the way, this passage into maturity was not marked by any special ceremony, as is done and sometimes overdone, today.) Along the way, he pointed out how the sunflowers faced towards the east. He told me to always remember that this was the way to Jerusalem. When we arrived at Ambover, we had a wonderful social gathering. We saw friends and relatives we hadn't seen for a whole year. In the evening, an animal was sacrificed and everyone partook of the joyous feast.

Often the Sigd festival was an occasion for matchmaking. Parents would arrange for young girls and boys – fifteen or sixteen years old – to be betrothed. The custom was that the girl would go to live in the boy's parents' home. After a few months of platonic living together, if she agreed to marry him, the groom's family made a big wedding lasting seven days in a large *succah* (hut). The groom had red and white bands placed around his head as symbols of peace and purity. The marriage was confirmed only when the bride was proven to be a virgin; then the *kes* blessed the couple. The groom wore a wedding band, *keshera* (meaning "tied"), to show that he was bound to his wife. He gave gifts to her family and the young couple went off to build their own home. The commitment to the marriage was quite equal. Should the situation arise, either the husband or the wife could get a divorce and thus become free. Usually, however, in case of separation, the children stayed with the mother.

Years later, when I came to Israel, my friends and I organized a Sigd festival to show solidarity with the people back home. Today this holiday has become very popular. The older folks fast, but the younger ones don't. We had planned our first celebration to be at the *Kotel Hama'aravi* (the Western Wall), but I hadn't realized that from this vantage point a large cross on a church and a shiny dome on a mosque came into view. These symbols were anathema to my primitive kinfolk. So we left that hallowed place and went off to the woods to carry out our festivities just like we used to in Ethiopia. To this day the Israeli Sigd festival is held among those trees.

Chapter III

When I turned five, "Abba" hired a tutor for me, a Christian who had studied Hebrew in Faitlovitch's school in Addis Ababa. He taught me to read the Bible in Hebrew and to learn the prayers by heart. Though Grandfather's diabetes caused him to be virtually blind, he knew the whole Bible by heart and corrected me every time I made a mistake. I used to relive all the biblical stories and loved every one of them. They were an integral part of my life, shaping my understanding of the world. While herding cattle, I used to imagine the places around me to be biblical settings. I'd wonder, "Was this the spot, beside the mountain, where David fought Goliath?"

I started school when I was nine, and one day that first year, I became very sick. I felt weak and tired and wanted to sleep all the time. I believe now that I had diabetes then, because I get similar symptoms today, when my blood sugar is out of control. Grandfather hired Aleka Melaku, a highly regarded Christian doctor, to come and heal me. He stayed in our house for three months trying to cure me. He used to boil all kinds of herbs, leaves, and roots in water, then cool the concoction down. When it was very cold, he'd pour it over my head early in the morning when the outside temperature was near freezing. I couldn't take it – it was much too cold for me! Finally, out of desperation, they tied me down and forced me to stay put while they doused me. One day I said I was okay and declared that I didn't need the treatment any more. As soon as they released me, I hurled myself out of the house, rolled down to the riverside and hid in the bushes. They searched all over; the men even crossed the river, but couldn't find me. Many people concluded that the Devil must have taken me into the river.

My great-grandmother, who couldn't keep pace with the others, stopped to rest near my hiding place, so I touched her feet. She screamed! But after she saw that it was me, she sobbed from relief and called everyone to come. Now everybody – except "Abba" – was sure that there was something really wrong inside me. They realized that I had a very strong will and were convinced that my body was possessed by evil spirits. Grandmother, like many Africans around her, believed in witchcraft and decided that we had to see a witch doctor. Grandfather was dead set against it, because he felt that witchcraft is against our religion. But Dr. Aleka Melaku had given up in despair and so Grandmother prevailed.

I was taken to a woman witch doctor's compound, from which I couldn't escape. I was confined there for nine months. Only Grandmother, Mother, and a cousin came to see me. "Abba" refused to visit. He didn't want to participate in any way in this pagan ritual. I missed him terribly. The "diagnosis" was that I had evil in my head, which made me sick. The witch doctor devised a "treatment" to get the evil out of me. She claimed that evil resides in the river and when I used to cross over to bring lunch to the men working on the other side, I neglected to throw some of the food into the river for the water creatures. That's why they caught me and made me sick. I don't remember what this "doctor" did to me. All I know is that when I came home, I had forgotten everything I had learned before. Grandfather became very upset when I couldn't remember the Torah and Psalms I used to recite by heart. Nevertheless, he was so relieved and happy that I was well.

Chapter IV

"Abba" was very much aware of the schemes of the European Christian missionaries. Many tried very hard to reach him, in particular, because they knew that if they converted him – the leader of the community – then the rest would follow suit. Others, especially the Seventh-day Adventists, made a great effort to lure our poverty-stricken children with promises of food and clothing. They'd usually make their push on Shabbat, when we were all assembled together. Grandfather took great pains to stop the proselytizers from crossing the river into our village, but it was a constant struggle to keep them away. Although we were at a disadvantage, "Abba" was determined to protect himself and us by strengthening his resolve to maintain our traditions and to practice our religion diligently. He respected everybody, but did not let anyone infringe on his personal beliefs. By keeping that kind of distance, Grandfather was able to sustain good relations with the neighboring Christian community.

Sometimes, however, conflicts arose. For example, at midday all the cattle from the surrounding villages used to come to the river to be watered. The Christians didn't want us Jews to go to the upper part of the river where the water was cleanest and "soil" it for them further down. The boys herding the cattle gave us a really rough time. One day I came back crying and Grandfather told me that if I came home crying again, I would not be allowed into the house. He said that whenever you have no reason to feel guilty, you have to challenge your attackers. From then on we kids learned, by playing war games, to fight to win. We fought so fiercely that we never lost a battle after that. Finally the parents of both groups, including "Abba," had to get together to cool things down. Those boys didn't ever bully us again.

I remember that one day the governor came with a representative to all the villages, including ours, and ordered everyone to provide him with wood to build his palace in Gondar. Now, Grandfather had a precious eucalyptus tree that he had nurtured for a long time. (Ages ago, an Australian had given the king a eucalyptus tree as a gift and then the seeds were replanted in Addis Ababa. "Abba" had collected some seeds from those trees and planted them in his garden.) We called this tree "the overseas tree." The governor fell in love with that tree the moment he saw it and commanded, "Cut it!" "Abba" tried to plead with him to save it, but to no avail. Grandfather cried all the time he chopped it down. This was the first time I had ever seen Grandfather cry. I was so distressed that I clung to his leg.

I never forgot this incident and kept promising myself that I had to find this governor and give him a piece of my mind. Some twenty years later I had the opportunity to meet him in Gondar – he was an old man then. When I confronted him with the story, he couldn't have cared less. He said that he did what was customary; he collected what was his due and had no qualms about my grandfather's feelings. These, he said, were the qualities that made him a good governor.

"Abba" told me that one day I would be carried on the wings of a bird to Jerusalem, just as it happens in the song we used to sing as children, "*Hassidah* come close to me and carry me to Jerusalem." Before Yom Kippur we always used to throw seeds in front of us in order to lure the stork to come to us and fly us to Jerusalem. That dream was an integral part of my life.

When I was nine, Grandfather predicted that one day I would marry a white woman and that I would travel all over the world.

Chapter v

When I was eleven (in 1955), one of Faitlovitch's students, a member of our own Bet Yisrael, Yona Bogale, and Rabbi Shmuel Be'eri, of the Jewish Agency's Department of Torah Education and Culture in the Diaspora, came to our village to discuss with my family the possibility of my going to Jerusalem to study. This was the first time in my life that I had ever seen a white man; I was dumbstruck. Was this the sign of the coming of the Messiah? Grandfather said that it was a great honor to be chosen to go to Israel. I would become one of the pioneers and future leaders of our community. I had mixed feelings about leaving. I loved my grandfather so much; I feared being separated from him. On the other hand, I was thrilled at the prospect of journeying to the Holy City.

I was one of fifteen children – eleven boys and four girls – selected to go from Ethiopia to Jerusalem. We walked the twenty kilometers from our village to Gondar. From there we had to fly to Addis Ababa. Of course, I had never flown before. I was very curious, yet frightened! The plane was like a big bird – I couldn't understand that it was built by human beings. I kept worrying that the plane would fall down. I breathed a sigh of relief when we finally landed safely.

We were obliged to spend six months in Addis Ababa until

all our documents were processed for permission to leave. Fortunately I stayed with a relative, Tadesse Yaacov (another of Faitlovitch's students), but, although his family treated me very kindly, I was terribly homesick. It might have taken much longer, but the red tape was speeded up by Yona Bogale, and by Tadesse Yaacov, who was now a government minister, as well as by the clandestine help of still another of Faitlovitch's students, the French professor Tamrat Emanuel, who was then out of favor with the emperor. Tadesse Yaacov managed to convince Haile Selassie to grant us our permits. When these were in order, we were summoned to the great palace.

A large car came to pick me up with some of my friends. We were taken to a huge ornate gate, which was opened on our behalf. Our eyes nearly popped out of our heads when we saw the sumptuous surroundings. At last we came before the great emperor, who was seated on a luxurious chair. Everyone was in awe. I, however, was more fascinated with his little brown dog. I couldn't stop looking at him. I had never seen such a small dog before. Haile Selassie graciously blessed us while we bowed before him and he commanded us: "Go get an education and come back to help our country!"

Professor Tamrat Emanuel took us from Addis Ababa to Asmara, Eritrea. The three-day bus trip was unbearably hot, bumpy, and altogether uncomfortable. Furthermore, we were cautioned to be wary of bandits. We stopped to eat at some strange places and I remember that one time I was served a plate of spaghetti. Believing it was full of squirming worms, I refused to eat it.

In Asmara we were met by Rabbi Shmuel Be'eri. He couldn't travel with us, because he had only an Israeli passport and was not allowed to fly into Muslim countries with it. Our group traveled with our Ethiopian papers from Asmara to Sudan, from Khartoum to Egypt, and from Cairo to Athens. Before one of the takeoffs, a lady got onto the plane wearing a fur coat. This was the first time I had ever seen someone in fur. I shied away from her, wondering,

"What kind of creature is this, half human and half animal?" She tried to talk to me, but I didn't understand her. She offered me something hard, wrapped in paper – I found out later that it was a candy – but I didn't eat it, fearing it wasn't kosher. As a matter of fact, none of us ate any of the food on the plane, because we didn't know if it was kosher.

Rabbi Be'eri met up with us in Athens. From there we all flew together to Israel. (Years later Rabbi Be'eri was convicted of stealing from the funds he had raised to help our cause.)

It is hard to describe the emotional feelings we had when we saw the land of our forefathers from the air. The excitement of actually coming to Israel was overpowering. When we finally landed, we bowed down and kissed the holy soil.

We were soon taken to a boarding school at Kfar Batya, near Ra'anana. The first group of Ethiopian kids had arrived there in 1955 and we came a year later. Our group consisted of: Akiva Eliahu, Dan Bedgilene, Moshe Rachmin, Eliahu Avimelech, Eliahu Sandeke, Tirza Alimeleh, Rachel Wube, Yaffa Wasse, Worat Mekuria, Yitzchak Adiche, Zakai Tadesse, Joseph Zavadia, Matti Elias, Simcha Gembar, and me, Baruch Tegegne. At last we found people we could talk to and who could give us moral support. Although we knew how to read and write Biblical Hebrew, we did not know Modern Hebrew, so the school sent us to an *ulpan*, a school that specializes in teaching modern Israeli Hebrew. Being immersed in this foreign language and living in a strange environment was difficult for us, but we soon learned enough Hebrew to go to regular classes and mix with the rest of the students.

Unfortunately, the Israeli kids never ceased to ridicule and torment us. How depressing it was for us to discover their racial prejudice! They laughed at our black skin and pulled at our curly hair. We had many fights with our schoolmates. After having been abused by Christians back home, I never thought I'd have to do battle with my Israeli brothers. Very often our older compatriots, like big brothers, had to come to our rescue. It was during one of these altercations that I broke my thumb. It has never healed. It is a constant reminder of the early struggle that is still going on and is so painful.

At home I had learned Torah through love; at this school they taught us by rigid strictness. I objected to that kind of hard discipline and stubbornly refused to comply. I was constantly being punished and was compelled to do many unsavory menial tasks. One day I was ordered to clean a large section of the synagogue before services. I balked. I said it wasn't fair for me to do the whole job by myself. The student in charge tried to force me to do it, but when I continued to refuse, he slapped me across the face. I wanted to beat him up, but he was big and tall and I was a slight fourteen-year-old. So I picked up a basket and threw it in his face. He came towards me, wanting to slap me again, but I jumped up and hit him, breaking my finger in the process. He pulled me by my sore hand and insisted I do my work. I still refused, I was so mad. Later I told Tadesse Yaacov's son what had happened. He became very incensed when he heard that a big brute had attacked a smaller boy. Next day he came and beat up my nemesis. I was happy that I had been avenged.

At that time a very serious change came over me. I had always identified religion with my wonderful grandfather and his goodness. I rejected the "religion" of this school, where my life was made miserable, and so I categorically refused to go to prayers. All I could think of was that one day I would become a pilot, fly back to Ethiopia, and bring back my "Abba" to be with me. Also, I was jealous of the other kids when their families came to visit. My heart ached for my loved ones who were so far away. I soon found a job on weekends and holidays to earn some money and to be away when the other families were there.

Once, when I was on a bus, little children started to call me names: "*Cushi, Cushi*" (equivalent to "nigger, nigger"). One of the mothers was near me and I asked the child, "What is your mother's name?" He said, "*Ima* (Mother)." "But," I said, "what name do others call her?" He didn't know. So I said to his mother, "Isn't it a shame that your child knows how to say '*Cushi*' before he knows your name?"

Outside the compound, when I appeared wearing a *kippah*, boys would harass me. They found it incongruous that I could be both black and Jewish. So I gave in and removed my skullcap whenever I left the premises.

The only good things that helped me survive my misery were our *madrichim* and *madrichot* (counselors) at the boarding school, who were very sympathetic and understood our feelings. I especially remember Rifka, an American, who really loved us and whom we loved in return. I also had a wonderful gardening teacher named Avraham, who took a particular interest in me. Fortunately I had a very good memory and was able to achieve fairly good grades in my classes.

During the 1956 War (the Sinai Campaign), there were times when we had to go down into a bunker for protection. I became very intrigued with the army. When I was a little older, I wanted to join GADNA (Israeli army training), but was not allowed to, because I wasn't an Israeli citizen. I was very upset. I pleaded with the director of our school, Mr. Dasburg, to do something to help me. He pulled some strings and, in a while, I was allowed to enroll. I spent the two summer months of my holiday in training and surprisingly, I turned out to be a good shot and was awarded a special medal.

Israel still did not recognize us Ethiopians as bona fide Jews. The rabbis insisted that we undergo a symbolic conversion. To complete this formality, they conducted us to a *mikvah* (ritual bath), where we were immersed in water, to "purify" us. (It was so warm and soothing in the *mikvah*, that I was reluctant to come out.) Then they inserted a needle and withdrew a few drops of our blood, to correspond to a ceremonial circumcision. And after all this humiliation, we still were not accepted.

Every year on Yom Ha-Atzma'ut (Israeli Independence Day), or on other special occasions, we were invited to President Yitzchak Ben-Zvi's house to celebrate with him. He was very interested in "the lost tribes" and encouraged us to maintain our Ethiopian culture and traditions. He couldn't, however, interfere on our behalf. His position was ceremonial, not political.

Baruch, age fourteen, in Israel

Baruch's group in Israel with Yona Bogale, c. 1958

Chapter VI

Our group was split up when we went to high school. Some went to Ayonot, near Rehovot. One other Ethiopian and I were sent to Neve Amiel in the Haifa area. Again we were faced with teasing and ridicule from the students. One day, a teacher asked me to organize the kids for a field trip. When I asked the students to get into line, one of the boys sassed back and said that he wasn't going to take orders from a Cushi! I snapped and beat him up. When the director called me to his office, I told him that the boy had embarrassed and insulted me. I had never called him Whitey; why should he call me names? In Ethiopia we took people just as they were. We were taught that you mustn't hurt others because we know how bad it feels to be hurt ourselves. And to top it off, there was a teacher who told me to take a steel brush and use strong soap and warm water to wash off all the black from my skin.

Upon graduating high school, I wanted very much to go on to university. I met with Mr. Halperin, head of Youth Aliyah, to discuss my plans, and to ask for continued financial assistance to go on with my studies. He turned me down. He said that I already had enough education to go back to the "bush and animals" of Ethiopia and that I could even become a minister there. He convinced me that I didn't really need a higher education. What I did need was more farming experience. So he sent me to the Hashomer Hatzair kibbutz Bet Alpha, where I was put to work driving a tractor and a bulldozer. The family of Gideon Eilat sponsored me and looked after me very well. I was wholeheartedly accepted by this communal farm, especially by the older members. I enjoyed being there and remained with them for a whole year. The kibbutz wanted me to stay on, but I had little contact with younger people and missed having friends my age. I left the kibbutz and got a job building the port in Ashdod. I earned quite a bit of money there by working twelve hours a day.

After I'd been in Israel for eight years, the Jewish Agency called me and asked me to go back to Ethiopia along with the rest of my group. Some of the kids didn't want to return. It was a tough decision for me, too. It was hard for me to leave the new comrades I had made at work, one of whom was an Arab, Tofik Bliyad, who became a lifelong friend. After much soul-searching, I agreed to go back. I was anxious to see my grandfather, my mother, and the rest of my family. Eight of my group of fifteen returned to Ethiopia from Israel in 1964, via Iran and Kenya. En route, I was devastated to learn that my beloved "Abba" had died the year before.

I returned to my homeland with the specific intention of teaching in the Jewish community. However, when Yona Bogale and some of the older students greeted us at the airport, they informed us that the school my grandfather had built was no longer there. It had been burned to the ground by the Christians. Furthermore, there was no money available to rebuild the school or to finance our teaching. We had to look for other work opportunities. But first, we were obliged to go and revisit Emperor Haile Selassie in his palace to thank him for having sent us to Israel.

I stayed in Addis Ababa and started to feel very lonely. Yona tried his best to care for us and offered us much warmth and kindness, but what did he really know about what we had gone through? I longed to visit my family. But how could I do that? I had no money to buy them presents and I could not come to them empty-handed.

This, according to Ethiopian custom, was never done. I was so distraught; I wanted to go back to Israel.

Some of us applied to the Ministry of Agriculture for jobs, but in order to be considered for a government job one needed to have a sponsor. Yona Bogale sponsored three of my friends and they were hired right away. He thought that with my family connections – a few of my relatives had government jobs – I could easily find my own sponsor. But I was too far away from anyone I knew.

I presented my documents to the government and the official was incredulous: "You went to study Torah and you know agriculture?" He was very officious and looked down his nose at me. As I had been away for so long, I had forgotten the Ethiopian protocol and didn't kowtow to him, nor pay him the "proper" respect. Needless to say, he didn't accept my application. At last my cousin, Tadesse Yaacov, now a government minister, came back from abroad and agreed to sponsor me. When I walked into the government offices with him, the place went into a flutter. It turned out that my cousin was the former minister of agriculture and the bureaucrat who had been so nasty to me got his comeuppance. Nevertheless, I had to pass a special test and – although I passed with flying colors – I still had to wait a whole month until I got the job.

I was penniless. Staying at a modest hotel, I couldn't pay the rent. One day the landlady said to me, "You say you were in Jerusalem. Did you bring back any holy water?" I replied, "Oh, yes, I brought some for my whole family." Whereupon I went to my sink, filled up a bottle of water and gave it to her. She was so ecstatically happy that she let me stay on rent-free.

My work took me far away to the Kaffa region. I was hired to teach agro-mechanics at the Gimma Agricultural and Technical School, funded by the American and Ethiopian governments. I was the only Jew at that school. I had told the American director, Dr. Warren, my whole history and he asked if I'd like to meet a Jewish anthropologist, who was there doing research on the local tribes and was endowed by the Rockefeller Foundation.

I was delighted to be introduced to this religious man the day he came to see my boss. He wore a *kippah* and made it clear that he did not work on the Sabbath. He was happy to meet me, too, and later took me to visit his wife and children, who lived in the city while he was out in the bush doing his research. He asked if I'd like to drive him to his destination, and then bring the car back to chauffeur his children to school and his wife to do her shopping. I was glad to be of service to them. On Shabbat I would spend a quiet day with the family and at sundown, he and I used to perform the *Havdalah* service (the prayer and ceremony that separate the holy Sabbath from the work week). I couldn't believe my good fortune in finding a soul mate amid the surrounding ocean of strangers.

Chapter VII

When Egypt, Syria, and Jordan attacked Israel in 1967, I couldn't sleep. I kept the radio glued to my ear all night. The reporter gleefully (and mistakenly) announced that the Egyptians had conquered Israel and were going to have breakfast in Tel Aviv and lunch in Jerusalem. The Ethiopian Muslims were dancing in the streets. I was crestfallen, for without Israel, life was meaningless for me. I was so pained to see all the jubilation and rejoicing that I felt a strong urge to make those people feel as much pain as I did.

At that time I had three close Christian friends who cherished Israel and Jerusalem as holy Christian sites. At first they also reveled in the reported defeat of Israel. They, too, were not really happy about the Jews having their own state. I explained to them that this time the Muslims were attacking my people, but the next time it could be theirs. They soon saw the logic of my argument. We decided to go out and burn up some Muslim stores. We came to a music store and asked the proprietor if he had any Israeli products. He said the only Israeli thing he had was a nail that was used to hang Jesus Christ.

Since I had been earning a fair salary as a teacher, I used to help some of the street children by buying them food, taking them to movies, paying for their education, and so on. They admired me very much. I commissioned them to set fire to the store, which they gladly did. They were never caught.

After the festive demonstrations, I went to the chief of police, and asked him why they allowed the citizens of Ethiopia to celebrate openly the victory of a Muslim country. I added that if Emperor Haile Selassie, who called himself "The Lion of Judah," heard about this, he would not tolerate it. After this visit, the chief of police and I became friends. I often walked with him to different stores and people didn't trouble me, because they thought I had a lot of influence with the authorities.

It took only six days until my friends and I were able to celebrate Israel's incredible victory over its invaders. The Israelis had counterattacked and conquered the Sinai, the Gaza Strip, the Golan Heights, and the West Bank of the Jordan. They also reunited Jerusalem, which had been divided since the State of Israel was established in 1948.

Chapter VIII

After the 1967 Six-Day War I wanted very much to go back to Israel and study at the Technion. I went to the Israeli embassy to plead with the ambassador to send me there, or at least to find me a job with an Israeli company in Ethiopia. I left an application with the Israeli Amiran Company in Addis Ababa to participate in an agricultural project I knew they were initiating. They couldn't hire me just then, but a few months later I received a wire saying they had something for me. The company, in cooperation with the Food and Agricultural Organization of the United Nations (FAO), was about to do some important market research and they felt I could be of use to them.

Three experts would be coming from Israel and they wanted me to spend a month with them gathering data from different farms as to their needs regarding tools, equipment, seeds, fertilizers, etc. I readily agreed to go along. We all met at the airport. The director of the FAO in Ethiopia – the Israeli Gershon Levy – and an Israeli official flew together on one plane. A chemical adviser, a machinery expert, an irrigation specialist, and I were on another Cessna.

Soon after takeoff, a violent storm erupted and our pilot decided to turn back and wait for the weather to clear. The other plane, however, continued on its course. Before long it crashed into a mountain. Gershon Levy, though seriously injured, survived. Unfortunately the Israeli official lost his life.

When we finally reached our destination, we embarked on a week of visiting various farms. Some of the larger ones were owned by Italians. Our market research proved to be useful; the Amiran Company was able to apply much of the information we had collected to plan future production and sales.

My contract with Amiran was up and I had to go back to my old job at the agricultural school. But how could I justify my month's absence? With some persuasion, I managed to get a letter from a doctor explaining that I had been ill all this time. I felt guilty for having deceived the company, but I felt a moral obligation to help Israel.

Chapter IX

While I was teaching at the school, my director read in the newspaper that an Israeli company was having an exhibition of farm equipment in Addis Ababa. He told me that he was interested in buying some new machinery for the school and asked if I'd like to see what they had. I jumped at the opportunity. He gave me a letter of introduction and I was on my way. I was flattered that the director trusted my opinion. This was a prestigious affair; Emperor Haile Selassie officiated at the opening ceremonies.

At the show I was greeted by Shmuel Halpern, who seemed to be very impressed by my credentials. He understood the importance of exposing all their agricultural products to a representative of a school from which graduates would go on to manage large farms. Making me knowledgeable of their line would be advantageous to their company. Mr. Halpern told me that a Mr. Zahavi, who was to arrive at four that afternoon, would show me around and answer all my questions. When I was about to leave, I said "*todah rabba* (thank you)." He was shocked to hear me speak Hebrew. I told him my story.

I was delighted to see Shaul Zahavi. I remembered him as being part of Gershon Levy's entourage when I was involved in the previous research project. He recognized me and gave me a grand tour, explaining everything in detail. It was fascinating. They had huge state-of-the-art tractors and bulldozers and a variety of other innovative machinery, as well as new kinds of fertilizers and seeds. He gave me a catalog to bring back to Gimma to show to the neighboring farmers.

The company offered our school a donation of some valuable tools and machinery. Arrangements were made for the school director to come to Addis Ababa to meet the Israeli ambassador, who was to make an official presentation of the gift to the school, on behalf of the Israeli government.

Chapter x

Shaul Zahavi asked if I'd like to come and work for the Amiran Company, whose head office in Israel is the Koor Company. I responded that I would be very pleased to work for an Israeli company. At last I'd be doing something for Israel. I told him, however, that I would need a firm contract. I could not relive the torment I had gone through the last time I had left my job. He said he was going away for a month's vacation, but would contact me upon his return.

A month later Zahavi came by car to my school with a contract to work with him on his farm. I left with him for Addis Ababa without notifying my director, because it would have been a terrible hassle to disengage myself from my teaching job. Firstly, I'd have to wait until they found a replacement. And secondly, I'd have to get a release from my sponsor. In addition there would be all kinds of other bureaucratic delays. Though I knew it was not the right thing to do, I left without notice because I felt I would be pursuing my goal to do something important for Israel.

Our company was selling very well to the Ethiopians. They chose to buy from us instead of the Italian or British companies, because our products came from Jerusalem – from the Holy Land. After a couple of months, however, the company ran into trouble. It happened that the tractor parts had been purchased from Romania (in exchange for oranges and other produce) and assembled in Israel. But they were not designed to withstand the Ethiopian heat. Before long the tractors leaked oil and the farmers were furious. They began bringing them back and, although their money was refunded, they were terribly angry; they felt their trust had been betrayed.

Rude remarks flew back and forth. The Israelis didn't understand Ethiopian sensitivities. Swearing at people might be acceptable in Israel, but in Ethiopia it is a blatant affront to one's pride. The Israelis failed to appreciate the mentality of these proud people, who, as history proves, have never been conquered, though many foreign regimes have tried to do so. One time I had to put myself between a gun-toting insulted Ethiopian client and a trembling Israeli salesman. I knew the client wouldn't shoot me, a fellow Ethiopian, for fear that the incident might mushroom into an ongoing family feud.

In time, the company management made an effort to solve the problems with the tractors and they did manage to improve them. All the other tools and products were very good. I started a training program for agricultural students to teach them how to use our equipment, so that they would be more likely to buy from us when they went off to their jobs as farm managers.

Chapter XI

A s my work at the company settled into a relatively normal
routine, I was able to take some time off to visit my family.
I got to Gondar and then I had to rent a mule to get to my
mother's village. I was so excited to go back! The village, at first,
seemed pretty much the same, except the distances to deliver food
to our fathers and bring cattle to the river seemed so much closer
than they used to be when I was a child.

Then, when I observed how my people lived, I couldn't believe
how they survived in such horrible conditions. There were far too
many families crowded together on such a small tract of land. And
there was constant bickering over space; there wasn't enough land
to divide up for the children. The poverty was alarming. The little
ones were sick, with no medication and very little food. I found it
too heart-wrenching to stay there for any length of time. When I
left, all the villagers sadly followed me, pleading: "Don't forget us!
Don't forget us!" That image has never left my mind. I said to myself,
"If God will help me, I'll do something for them one day."

I had to return the mule, so I set out on foot, accompanied by
a few relatives, to meet four of my old schoolmates, who were now
teaching in Ambover. En route I met one of my sisters, Malefia. She
was returning from a school in Ambover, which she had attended
since the Christians had burned down our school in Wozaba. I

remembered her only slightly but thought about her very often. I became so emotional; I hugged her closely and cried tears of joy.

I also went to visit my father in his village. When I was at Gimma, I had met someone who knew Father and was able to tell him exactly where I was. Father and my half brothers, whom I had never met before, came to visit me there. He and I had joyously renewed our acquaintance then; this time I was introduced to his whole family. Here, too, conditions were disastrous. I became even more resolved to do something to help my people.

When I returned to Addis Ababa, I met with Yona Bogale, and discussed with him the possibility of finding some land to resettle my village. He thought there might be a chance of buying acreage somewhere to set up a collective farm, but we knew that we needed some outside assistance in achieving our goal. We remembered an Ethiopian army veteran, Ras Wibenech, who had vowed to help the Ethiopian Jews after he and his men had been saved by a unit of Falasha soldiers during the Italian Campaign (1935–41). He and Professor Bentwich (legal adviser to Haile Selassie) had formed the Falasha Welfare Association in England for that very purpose. We planned to approach them for assistance, as well as the pro-Falasha Committee for Ethiopian Jews in New York and the government of Ethiopia. Ras Wibenech agreed to speak to the authorities on our behalf.

We were soon given rights to a piece of land near the Sudanese border. My employers gave me permission to work with the new settlement. They let me use all the equipment I needed. Together with my family and other villagers, we started the arduous task of clearing the bush and building new houses. My kinfolk moved into this compound and before long the farm was thriving and my people were flourishing. Everyone felt great satisfaction in what we had accomplished.

Yona Bogale told me that a Jewish American aid worker, a Dr. Cohen, was in the vicinity charged with the task of helping the Ethiopians improve their economy. He suggested that if I helped this American with farming technology, he would probably assist us in our enterprise. It turned out that Dr. Cohen's office was quite close to one of my company's branch offices in Addis Ababa and I knew the area very well. It was in the district of Homera, in the village of Avedrafi. I was very happy to work with him. Eventually he bought equipment from my firm, which I got for him at a reduced rate.

Chapter XII

One day some Sudanese appeared at our settlement and began snooping around. We were scared. I selected three men – Fisseha Simon, Aba Chekole, and Aba Berhanu – and posted them on the top of three high hills to keep watch. On Friday, our *kes*, Wubeshet Ayetegeb, asked me to go with him to the river to bathe, as in a *mikvah*, in preparation for Shabbat. Suddenly, without warning, the Sudanese began shooting in such rapid succession that the mountains looked like they were up in smoke. I thought everyone had been killed. I got into my Land Rover and drove sixty-five kilometers to the police station for help, but the chief showed no concern whatsoever. He said, "I don't care." He didn't want to do anything to help the Jews.

In the meantime, Zemene Mekonin traveled on foot from the farm in Avedrafi to report to me that all the people were safe, except for the three watchmen. He didn't know what had become of them.

Next day I went to the military officer. He did feel sorry for us, but said he couldn't move his soldiers near the border without permission. He needed to send a telegram to get orders to do so. I prevailed upon him to come back with me because of the urgency of the situation and he finally agreed. He selected a few men to accompany him. My anxiety continued to mount as we traveled;

I didn't know what to expect. Imagine my relief when I found everyone safe and sound.

As Zemene Mekonin had testified, the three watchmen were nowhere to be found. It turns out that their bravery had turned back the Sudanese invaders and saved our people from being massacred. We learned later that, while shooting at the Sudanese, they had used up all their bullets, but left one each in case they had to commit suicide. These local heroes had killed five people, one of whom was a very high-ranking officer. Luckily, they were able to escape through a valley in a roundabout way – even going through Sudanese territory – until they came back home. We were thankful that nobody in our community had died. Our *kes* remarked that the lone cloud that had appeared over our farm was a sign that God was protecting us.

Trusting God was not enough. I went off to speak to the chief of the area, Wakshim Newette, from whom we had bought our land. He was the landowner of the neighboring settlement and agreed that if the Sudanese did this to us today, they could do it to him tomorrow. He sent his whole population out to support us. They came with guns and were ready to defend us against the Sudanese. The military personnel who had come with us blocked our way and wouldn't let us move. We all sat down and held our ground. It was so hot and the military men so uncomfortable that finally they couldn't take it any more. The officer sent for the police to relieve them. This defused the situation and the police told us all to go back home.

When we returned, we were devastated to find that our farm had been destroyed by the Sudanese. Our neighbors helped us temporarily with food and clothing. Now my people, yet again, were in dire straits.

The Sudanese accused us of building an Israeli military base on their border. It was obvious that they would not let us live in peace. I told Yona Bogale in Addis Ababa what had happened and he was very upset. He approached Dr. Cohen, the American aid worker, to see what he could do. I appealed to the central defense minister, General Nega Tegegne, who was married to Haile Selassie's daughter. (General Tegegne was no relation to me and not even Jewish, but I knew him well as he and I came from the same province, Gondar. I used our common name to get out of a tight spot later.) The minister said he couldn't do anything until they investigated all the issues.

The officials were divided. Some believed the map showed that the mountain was exactly on the border, but that the land we had cultivated was traditionally on the Ethiopian side. Others argued that our whole farm was in Sudan. In any case, the Sudanese were on our backs and everyone feared that this conflict might spark a war. We didn't have enough manpower nor were we sufficiently armed to defend ourselves.

In the end, we Ethiopian Jews left this farm to the Sudanese people. The landlord, Wakshim Newette, felt he had made a big mistake by selling us that parcel of land. However, as a gesture of support, he gave us another tract of land in the same area, but further toward the interior, at a safe distance from the Sudanese border. My village moved there and began to work the new terrain.

At that time, I had to go back to Addis Ababa to resume working for my company. Akiva, a friend who was with me at Kfar Batya, came to take my place to help the people resettle. Some of the Christian neighbors – even those who had previously supported the Jews – opposed the resettlement and continued their harassment.

The farmers in the surrounding area used to bring their grain to be ground at a mill, which we Jews had bought. Sometimes the atmosphere became so bitter that irate Christians would hold a gun to the Jewish miller, force him to grind his grain, and then refuse to pay.

Things became so bad that one day some Christians kidnapped Akiva and took away his gun. Fortunately he was able to escape and run off to Gondar. In spite of all these troubles, the Bet Yisrael persevered and continued to live there and develop their communal farm.

Chapter XIII

No sooner did I get back to my company than they sent me to work at a large farm in Metema, whose owner had bought our machinery and equipment and he needed somebody to teach his men how to assemble and operate them. The only way to get there was by plane in the summertime. When I finished my job at that farm, I couldn't get out! It was winter and too rainy for planes to land there. My employers sent me a telegram saying that the farm owner wanted to hire me to manage the farm and that they (the company) would guarantee my salary. I stayed on for another four months. I taught the men modern methods of cultivation, how to use the new machinery, and which seeds to plant for maximum yield. At harvest time, we were happy to see that the farm produced approximately four times its previous output. The farmer wanted me to stay on and manage his farm. He offered me a good salary, a house, a car, expenses, and 10 percent of the profit. But I felt obliged to go back to my employers.

When the skies finally cleared, a plane arrived and took me back to Addis Ababa. I began working for the company again and I soon found myself wrestling with another dilemma. Though I liked my job very much, I kept wondering, "What can I do to help support my family?" You see, the farm I had managed before, in Metema, was just 250 kilometers away from my people. From this company in Addis, the distance was some 750 kilometers. I weighed the pros and cons and decided to leave the company and return to manage the farm. I worked for the landowner one more year. From there I was able to visit the settlement and reunite with my family and my people. I even saw my father again and became closer to him and his new family.

At last, I saw an opportunity to buy my own farm (from a private landlord) and become independent. As I was now quite expert in modern agriculture, I planned to have a model farm and to serve as an advisor to the surrounding farmers.

I purchased a large farm, and slowly my relatives started to come to help me cultivate it, while I provided them with food and shelter. We rented a horse-drawn plow and borrowed the landowner's tractor on Sundays, on his day of rest. Before long, I was able to buy my own tractor and jeep.

The Zahavi brothers, Shaul and Amnon, rented a farm not too far from mine. It was good to have neighbors nearby with whom to exchange visits.

I saw how my people enjoyed working the land, knowing that they themselves would benefit from the harvest and did not have to give a large percentage of it to the landowner. I then made up my mind to buy a larger tract of land, for I was determined to gather in all of Bet Yisrael onto our very own property.

Chapter XIV

During this period, the Zahavi brothers introduced me to Ambassador Hanan Aynor and First Secretary Itzhak Shalev, from the Israeli embassy, and Evron, the military attaché to Ethiopia, who invited me to go to Addis Ababa. There they told me that I was needed for a very important mission. They offered to "make my time worthwhile," but I said that if I were to help the State of Israel, I would do it for free. They told me that a friend of Israel, who lived in the southern part of Sudan and was an outspoken opponent of the present Sudanese government, was being threatened. His life was in danger. They wanted me to rescue him. I was told to be careful and especially to be discreet – not to let any authorities see him.

I agreed to take the job. I spent two weeks looking for the man, and at last, aided by some trusted friends, I located him and brought him back with me to Ethiopia. I cautioned him to keep his identity secret. We trekked through the countryside until we came to Gondar. All the while people kept asking: "Who is that man? "Where is he from? What is he doing here?" I explained that he was a Sudanese refugee, but I sensed that they were suspicious and whispering behind my back. Finally, the pressure became too much for me. I took him to the police general and told him that this man was seeking refugee status. He asked me if I could support him, and I said, "No problem." I felt it would be easier to move about with him if the police were on my side. Knowing that I had arranged to meet my Israeli contact in Bahr Dar (near the Nile headwaters), I mentioned to the officer that the "refugee" had confided to me that all his life he had dreamed of making a pilgrimage to the source of the Blue Nile and had asked me if I could take him there. The general gave us the required permit.

I rented a Land Rover and went to our destination in a roundabout way to meet "Yossi," who announced that the ambassador and Evron were to meet us very soon. They were infuriated when they heard that I had taken the man to the police. They reminded me that I had strict orders not to let any authority see him. I, however, felt that I had to do what I thought was right to protect myself and my charge. I knew my country and the mentality of the Ethiopians. They, the Israelis, were directing from afar and didn't really understand what I was up against.

The next day our "refugee" told us that a missile site had been built near the Aswan Dam to protect it. Close by, on the Sudanese side, there was an armaments factory, built by Syria, Lebanon, Libya, and Egypt. I understood how threatening this must be to the State of Israel. The Israelis wanted me to try to convince one of the Sudanese officers – who would be adequately compensated – to come to them. I staunchly refused. They tried to prevail upon me to work for them full-time, but I resented the kind of blind obedience they demanded – to follow orders without question. I said my goodbyes and went back to my farm. I never saw the "refugee" again.

Chapter xv

threw myself into my new venture of resettling my people. I found the ideal spot. I sold my farm at a good profit and bought a much larger tract of land, with a river running through it. I planned to set up an irrigation system to guarantee sufficient water for the crops. We started to clean up the bush; one night, we were taken aback by the bone-chilling sound of a lion's roar. Next day we tracked him down and killed him.

Slowly I began moving my fellow Bet Yisrael onto the new farm. But the neighbors gave us no respite. They complained to the landlord, saying, "Why did the Jews – who become hyenas at night – come to take away our land?" The landlord told them that he didn't know we were Jewish. The Christians started to shoot into the air to frighten us away. The next morning, the landlord came to me and demanded that I pay him more money if I wanted to live in peace. I told him that that night I would turn into the biggest hyena he'd ever seen and I would come into his compound and eat up all his children. He laughed.

I convinced my people that we had to stop running and cowering from our persecutors. I bought the best guns I could find and armed all the men. In addition, I played politics. I hired the landlord's sons as bodyguards and armed one of them with a machine gun. I knew that the Christians would not fire at them and I also knew that, as custom dictated, they were honor-bound to protect me. This proved to be a very good idea. The neighbors stopped bothering us.

One day one of my cousins took out the tractor-trailer to transport several people from our area to another village. Along the primitive road, the vehicle ran into a huge bump at the top of a hill and turned over. The riders were thrown helter-skelter. As luck would have it, one of the passengers, a priest who ministered to the whole area, broke his leg in the accident. The others were so incensed they wanted to kill our whole community. A witness, who knew me well, ran all night to tell me what had occurred. I rushed out to check on my cousin, to see if he was still alive. I was informed that he had gone to the police station to tell them what had happened in order to protect himself against the violent passengers. They immediately put him in jail. When I arrived there I had to arrange for his release. I contacted some responsible people in the area for advice and they counseled me to take the priest to the hospital in Gondar, which I did, and paid for his complete medical treatment. I learned that you have to stand tall and not show any weakness.

Chapter XVI

One of the Christian neighbors kept infringing on our land. When we confronted him, he said, "What are you going to do, you Falasha?" My cousin was so angry, he threatened him, saying, "If you ever set your foot on my land, I will kill you!" This man had a cousin in Addis Ababa who knew about this conflict. One evening I saw him in a bar and went over to greet him. He retorted, "You Falasha, you make problems for my brother." I took out my gun, which I always carried with me, and said, "I'll show you what it means to be a Falasha." He continued to call me abusive names, so I shot a bullet in the air and told him, "This is a warning! If you insult me again, next time I will put the bullet in your head." Everybody flew out of the bar.

Next morning, there was a knock at my hotel room door. I opened it, and bang! The man I had threatened in the bar, my neighbor's cousin, shot me. I fainted. People rushed me to the hospital. When they took off my clothes, they discovered that a bullet had gone through the right side of my body – just above the waist – from front to back. The Yugoslavian doctor who was on duty that day said that he would have to operate, because there was too much blood accumulated in my wound. But another doctor came along and decided to pump the blood out through my nose. A relative of my attacker who had the right blood type donated blood to save my life, and coincidentally, also the life of my attacker, because if I stayed alive, he couldn't be accused of murder.

When the police came for me to identify my assailant, I told them that the man they had detained was not the person who had shot me. My first impulse was to take revenge myself. I figured that if he were sent to prison, I would have no satisfaction. Later I reasoned that: (a) we had been friends before, and (b) I had just wanted to scare him and he was drunk when he shot me. I didn't want to make him suffer a severe punishment.

His family became very appreciative of what I had done for him. A wealthy brother of his, who owned a large company, sent me money every month while I was unable to work. Other members of the family became big supporters of the Ethiopian Jewish people. A sister, proprietor of a large hotel in Gondar, was very solicitous to any Jewish traveler who happened to come her way.

Things quieted down after that and we had a peaceful year. There were about three hundred people working on the farm. I had earned the respect of the Jews and Gentiles as an established landowner. Finally, I began to feel very secure.

In addition, I started to do some – slightly risky – business with the Sudanese along the border. I bought such items as gum Arabic, sesame seeds, and spices from them at very good prices and resold them to the Ethiopians. News of my success spread rapidly and so did my reputation as a trustworthy trader. I became more powerful and was admired by the people in the area. My goal was to make my people take pride in themselves and stop feeling oppressed and depressed. I made a special effort to build up their self-esteem and to give them a good deal of moral support. By setting a good example, I tried to show them how to be strong and to be confident.

Chapter XVII

There are three main agroclimatic zones in Ethiopia. In the mountains is the *Dega* – meaning the cold area – where mostly wheat is grown. Between the mountains and the lowlands is the *Weyna Dega*, which has cold and hot weather, where three crops are grown. And then there are the lowlands, called *K'olla*, which are very hot and breed malaria and other tropical diseases. Most of the Jews came from the *Dega* or *Weyna Dega*. Few Ethiopians go to the *K'olla*, because of their fear of getting sick. If they do go there, it is for hunting or doing business with the Sudanese.

In the early 1970s, agriculture had just begun to be developed in the *K'olla* and people were coming from all parts of the country to invest in it. Our farm was in the heart of these lowlands. To avoid malaria, my workers and I took anti-malaria pills. Yet in Metema, people were dying every day from malaria or yellow fever or other liver infections, which they got from the polluted water. Nevertheless, Ethiopians still came to the *K'olla* from the highlands, hoping to make a decent living there. When they got sick many couldn't afford to go to the hospital – they were lying in the streets – so I put up a shelter for them. I paid the doctors to come and treat them and had my cooks prepare food for them, Jew and Gentile alike –

it made no difference to me. It was a *mitzvah*, the fulfillment of a commandment. Besides, it didn't cost much money to help them.

The sick were so grateful, they made up a poem for me in Amharic, which translates something like this:

> The people – we live in the dark,
> But Baruch is our light.
> Please, God, don't let him die.
> We'll try harder and harder to get well;
> In time we'll be blessed like Baruch, [the meaning of
> my name].

Many stayed in the shelter for three or four months convalescing. If someone died, I organized a respectful burial for him; for a Muslim, I'd call for an imam; for a Christian a priest; and for a Jew, a *kes*. I valued every individual and in return I made many friends. To this day, I meet people in different parts of the world who come up to me and say, "Are you Baruch? I remember when you…" I'm happy that I was able to help them when I could.

Chapter XVIII

I continued to run the farm, but one day I began to feel very ill. I didn't know what was happening to me. After a few days, my cousin took me to the hospital in Gondar, where the doctors discovered that I had diabetes. They told me what foods to eat and gave me pills to take. When I returned home, I took their advice and started to feel much better.

Life was gradually improving for us. All was going well until 1974, when the revolution broke out. Civil war erupted. The Dergue came to power and imprisoned Emperor Haile Selassie. There was no longer any government authority to maintain order. It was sheer anarchy.

We used to grow three main crops: sesame seeds, sorghum, and cotton. The sesame seeds ripened early and we paid our workers from the proceeds of their sale. The sorghum provided them with their food. The cotton was the only profit crop we had. As food shortages increased during the civil war, starving neighbors would sometimes kill for food, or turn the farmers in to the authorities. Together with other neighboring farmers, we had bought a cotton gin in Gondar, to which we brought our cotton for processing. We agreed to sell the cotton cooperatively at the best price we could get. The revolutionary regime took possession of our gin, froze everything, and never paid us the proceeds of the sales. Having no income, we found it next to impossible to go on living that way.

The rebels approached us and asked us to house several of their students, who were taking courses at nearby schools. They also used our tractors to move lumber to some of their construction sites. The feudal landlords, thinking we were supporters of the revolution, came to our farm and burned everything to the ground. Their sole purpose was to get us out of there. They also destroyed the Zahavi brothers' farm. Furthermore, the new government was against all faiths – Christian and Muslim as well as ours. They experimented with clamping down on religions by starting with us, because we were the weakest. They forbade Jewish education and Jewish religious practice. Intimidation escalated to the point where teachers in our villages were taken away and tortured.

Our situation in Ethiopia was hopeless.

SECTION 2
Wandering Jew

Chapter 1

B efore I had started farming in 1971, I had plenty of money, yet
I kept on dreaming of going back to Israel. When my mother
got wind of this, she sent word for me to come to the village
and begged me to stay there with her. (She was too ill at the time
for me to even think of taking her with me to Israel.) Now, in 1974,
after all our efforts to settle my people in a safe and prosperous
environment, the revolution erupted and I saw that there was no
future for us Jews in Ethiopia.

I believed that Israel was our only salvation. I was determined
to go there and do something to help my people. But, because
of the revolution, I wasn't able to leave the country legally – the
borders were closed – so I decided to escape to Sudan and try to
reach my destination from there. The day before I had planned to
leave, I gathered my family together and told them that I wanted
to have a family party, to boost our morale. I didn't tell them anything about my plans. All I told them was that I had to go to Sudan
to buy fuel, because the road between us and Gondar, where we

usually bought our supply, was cut off. A pall of gloom settled over the gathering – my family felt a sense of foreboding.

I took a little money with me and left the rest of what I had for my family, entrusted with my cousin, Eshete Feredeh, a strong individual, whom I authorized to take my place. I left with a heavy heart, yet with a strong conviction that Israel would come to our rescue.

To circumvent the ever-vigilant border guards, I had to trudge a long distance by foot to get to Sudan, all the way from Metema to Doka. It took me five days. When I finally got there, I met one of the men with whom I used to do business. Pretending to be on a buying trip, I discreetly asked him questions to find out what people were thinking about the changes that were taking place. From Doka I went to Gedaref, where I met up with another Christian acquaintance, who was in Sudan seeking asylum as a refugee. I discovered that the process of applying for residency in Gedaref entailed months in a detention camp and even then there was no guarantee that I would eventually get the permit.

After having examined all the possibilities, I decided to go to Khartoum, where I thought my chances for securing refugee status would be quicker. In order to move about freely in that city and perhaps find work, I needed papers. I was warned that if the police caught me without them, I could be sent to prison. Fortunately, my Christian friend kindly provided me with an escort, who took me to Khartoum by truck. The rickety vehicle was weighted down with merchandise and we, along with some other transients, were loaded on top of the pile. In a way, the clatter of that hazardous ride turned out to be a blessing. Because of the noise, we were unable to talk to each other, so no one could discover from my accent that I was a foreigner and report me to the authorities.

When we finally got to Khartoum, I went to the Ministry of the Interior to apply for a permit. I told them that I had relatives in Europe who were sending me money. I assured the clerk that I didn't need any help whatsoever and that I wouldn't be a burden to them. I lived frugally and prayed that nothing would go wrong. It took three months until I finally got the necessary papers to allow me to stay in that city.

Chapter 11

While in Khartoum, I met some other refugees. I made the acquaintance of two brothers who wanted to go to Sweden to visit another brother there. They had their papers, but didn't have enough money for transportation. Because they seemed to know their way around, I offered to get them money if they agreed to take me with them. I took one of the brothers with me and together we set off for Gedaref, to send a letter to my cousin via a merchant friend. I wrote my cousin, Eshete Feredeh, that I needed money very badly. I advised him to sell the guns and any cotton they might have. I also suggested that he bring the tractor across the border, where I could sell it quite easily.

I received a letter in response, including 75 *birr*, saying that he would try to get me more money next time, but a lot of our people refused to give up their guns. Unfortunately, when my cousin tried to bring the tractor across the border, he was caught. The tractor was confiscated and he was sent to prison. It created a big hassle and it cost a lot of money and manipulation to get him released.

While wandering around Gedaref, I feared for my life. I felt so trapped, I wanted to get out of Sudan by any means possible. I even tried to convince a friend of mine, who was an Ethiopian pilot, to hijack a plane with me and take me directly to Tel Aviv. Fortunately, he had more sense than I.

Feeling very low, I bumped into a merchant I knew, Al-Tzadik, who came from Doka. I wanted to hug him, in the Sudanese manner, but he pushed me aside and cried, "Don't touch me!" Someone had told him that I was going from there to Israel. He shouted, "You are an Israeli spy! You are a traitor and you are coming with me to the police." He grabbed my arm. Calmly, I said to him, "When you were at my house I treated you so well. You know me. Why do you think I am a spy?"

My mind was reeling. I was suddenly acutely aware of the incident that happened at the Bet Yisrael farm I had run near the border when my men killed five Sudanese men. The police might still have my name on record and then I'd be in real trouble. I refused to go. I struggled with him, for I knew that even if proved innocent, I could be kept in jail for three to six months, with no explanation. I begged him not to do it, but he was stronger than I. He shoved me into his car and locked the door. I asked him, "What can I do to stop you from taking me to the police?" He replied, "I know you are a wealthy man. You did business with black and white men, and obviously you got a lot of money from the Israeli government to set up your big farm. Give me 5,000 *birr*." I asked him to bring me back to my hotel so I could ask friends to lend me the money. Luckily, he agreed.

At the hotel, I contacted an Eritrean merchant friend, told him my story, and asked him for a loan. He was so infuriated when I told him what had happened that he jumped on Al-Tzadik, who denied that he had ever asked for a bribe and deceitfully said that he had come back to the hotel because he had forgotten something there. My friend let him go.

To struggle further would have made matters worse. I was left with no options but to return with the man from Doka to the police station. He took me to his brother-in-law, who was a high-ranking officer. This policeman said he couldn't do anything – it wasn't his department. He directed us to the officer in charge of immigrants, Colonel Ibrahim. At this point, instead of becoming more panicky, I became very calm. I felt that whatever happened, I would show no fear.

I walked with confidence into Ibrahim's office.. The merchant told him I was an Israeli spy – that he knew me from Ethiopia, where I ran a farm for the Jewish community. The colonel asked me if this was true. I said, "No, my mother was Ethiopian and my father was Sudanese. Do I look like a Jew? Have you ever seen a black Jew?" Colonel Ibrahim shrugged his shoulders. As we were the last item on his roster that day and it was unbearably hot, he told us to come back at 7:30 the next morning. I was given strict orders not to leave the hotel till then.

Chapter III

didn't want to go to prison, especially not in Gedaref! It wasn't even fit for animals, let alone for humans. If they sentenced me to jail, I'd kill myself. I felt I had to escape; it was my only choice.

When I was dropped off at the hotel I spoke to the hotel watchman, an Eritrean, who had seen what had happened to me and was sympathetic to my predicament. I asked him where I had to go to get out of the country. He gave me three choices: via Port Sudan, Uganda, or Chad. When I got to my room, I wrote each name on a scrap of paper, then threw them up in the air and prayed to the God of my Grandfather to help me choose the right one. Hesitantly, I picked up the one marked "Chad."

I went back to the watchman, swore him to secrecy, and asked for detailed directions to Chad. He mapped out an itinerary for me, and I spent the whole evening planning my escape. Then I wrote a letter to my cousin, explaining what Al-Tzadik had done to me. Approaching an Ethiopian acquaintance, Alam, who had arrived just a week earlier, I prevailed upon him to deliver it to my cousin. When I told him what had happened to me and about my plans to escape, he pleaded with me to take him along. "Okay," I said. "If one of us survives, he'll be able to tell the story."

For me it was a matter of life and death, but for him it was a matter of choice. Yet, if that was what he wanted, I was willing to go along with it. He came from a royal family and had fled the revolution with some money in his pocket. He was younger than I and didn't know Arabic, whereas I was able to speak enough of the language to communicate with the people in the area. Besides, I was the only person he knew there that he could trust.

Chapter IV

I delegated Alam to buy two *djellabas* (long hooded cloaks worn by many Middle Eastern men) and sent the watchman to buy two train tickets. The train was leaving at one A.M. from Gedaref to Khartoum. From there we were to transfer to another train that went towards Chad. The watchman got a taxi to pick us up behind the hotel and take us to the train. Wearing our disguises, we sat in the station, pretending to be very tired and half asleep, so that we wouldn't have to talk to anyone.

The second-class section of the train was very crowded. We decided to separate; in case one of us got caught, then the other would survive. To avoid detection of our nationality and speech (by our accents), we acted as if we were deaf mutes. People pushed and shoved us in all directions and it was hot as hell. The stench in our compartment was insufferable.

At the first stop, I motioned to Alam to follow me to the top of the train, where the poor people hitched rides. Nobody talks to you there and the air is much fresher. We climbed up the ladder, and found that the roof was not flat, but slanted to meet at a peak in the middle. We sat back to back, and tied our *djellabas* together, so that if one of us fell asleep, the other would keep him from falling off. At first this arrangement was scary, but soon we got used to the rhythmic motion of the train and managed to keep our balance.

At every stop we were surrounded by vistas of desert. People approached us selling fruit, sandwiches, and water. At one of these stations, I noticed an elderly couple who had been sitting close to us on top of the train. I wanted to ask them some questions, but Alam was paranoid; he was afraid they'd betray us. I assured him that these old people would do us no harm. I went over to them and asked if they knew how to get into Chad from the train stop at the border. By coincidence they were going back home to Chad after having been on a jihad to Mecca.

I told them that we were from war-torn Eritrea, on the border of Sudan, and that we were escaping because we were Muslims and our home had been destroyed. Introducing ourselves with assumed Muslim names, I explained that we were going to visit our brother in Chad. The old man said, "Don't worry, we will guide you."

When the train stopped at Ne'ala, in the Darfur region, we got off with our new guides and went to a café where we treated them to some tea and sweets. Then they took us to a truck stop, where we were to get onto a truck that was going to the Chad border. Again the crowds were incredible –people were being heaped on top of heavily loaded vans. There was no law stipulating how much payload a vehicle could carry. The truckers wanted to get as much money as possible, so they piled on as many people as they could.

Sitting on the top of the truck, I was jostled by the man next to me, but couldn't fight back. I was always afraid of being found out. The bumpy, uncomfortable ride seemed to last forever. To top it off, our truck broke down and the driver had to wait hours for another one to come along with spare parts. Finally a friend of his arrived with the necessary pieces and he was able to fix it. It took nearly two weeks of plowing through the desert of Sudan till we came near the border. The elderly man told us that they were getting off at the next stop, which was closer to their home in Chad. He informed us, however, that after they left, the vehicle was going to pass through a military camp where the guards would stop us to check our papers. He instructed us to tell the driver to let us off *before* the military camp, at a certain teashop, in a small village called Genina. The driver categorically refused, saying that he was not allowed to stop there. If he were caught, the authorities would accuse him of smuggling and would take away his license. The elderly man said, "Bribe him."

Chapter v

The driver asked for a lot of money. I gave him what I had. He said, "When I stop, you and your friend jump out and mix with the crowd." To our surprise, a lot of others jumped off at the same stop. I, however, reminded the driver that we were the people who paid him, and held on to him insisting that he take us to the teashop and introduce us to the owner. Reluctantly he led us there and then took off in a hurry.

The local Sudanese, hired by the government to guard the borders, were very active there. They patrolled the border and were out to catch smugglers. Just after we arrived at the teahouse, we saw a troop of horsemen bearing bows and arrows, charging down the road. The proprietor, knowing we were in danger, hid us under a bed. I could barely breathe. The owner, when questioned, pointed back toward the bush and told the guards, "They went that way." The men rode off in a hurry.

When we emerged, the owner gave us a cup of tea and asked us our plans. He told us that his son would come that night to take us across the border – for a certain fee. Fortunately Alam still had some money.

The boy came in the middle of the night riding on a donkey. That day, Alam had had an accident; somehow a sharp piece of dry wood had penetrated the back of his knee. It was bleeding so profusely, I had to tear up my shirt to make him a bandage. I told him that we were compelled to leave, no matter how bad he felt; there was no choice. I got him to hold on to me so I could help him walk, while we followed the donkey and its rider as best we could. It was incredibly dark and I marveled at how the donkey knew the way. After a while we passed behind the military base. Alam and I were terribly exhausted, but the boy pushed us onward.

By midday, it was so hot that our eyes got bleary and irritated. We just had to stop. At a shady spot under some trees we lay down for a little while. But before we were able to relax, the boy prodded us with his stick, and said, "Hurry up! We have to go. I must get home tonight. If you don't want to go, you can stay right here."

Wearily, we pulled ourselves together and followed him to the home of a *m'alem Koran*, a teacher of the Koran. He was the key person involved in exchanging smuggled goods and people. He headed a big compound outside the village. We stayed with him for about a week until I started to recover my strength. But Alam's health was deteriorating. His wound was festering and he was afraid to eat the local food. I often sneaked out of our hiding place to buy him some milk and bread.

According to the plan, we were to be taken to Chad by a party of smugglers who were coming from Chad to Sudan with goods and/or people. This group of "merchants," introduced to us by our host, agreed to take us back with them. We negotiated a price, which included the cost of two camels on which we were to cross the Sahara desert. Six men showed up at around four A.M., when it is coolest, but with only one camel for the two of us. There was just one seat available, perched on top of the merchandise. Of course, Alam, who was very ill, got to sit while I plodded along on foot.

Chapter VI

The trek through the Sahara was extremely difficult. I had never in my life experienced such unrelenting heat. I was not prepared for it and hadn't dressed appropriately. The blazing sun made the desert seem on fire. It was agonizing. My eyes couldn't take the burning dryness. The dust scalded my face and lips, so that I was covered with blisters. I found it impossible to walk in the scorching sand. I felt I couldn't go on any longer. Besides, Alam's wound was getting worse and I had no way of alleviating it. I fell to the ground and told my companion that, for me, this was the end. He became so confused, he started to cry.

I stretched out on the sand, ready to die. When the others saw me lying there, they stopped and came to see what had happened. A buzz erupted among them. They didn't want to leave their "brother" there to die. One of them suggested that they take me to the next village, where the people might look after me. They went out of their way to carry me there. Alam tagged along.

Once we got there, I noticed that the villagers kept their water supply in a huge earthenware pot. I was desperately thirsty and begged for water, but they wouldn't let me drink too much. They said that if I drank a lot, I could die. They washed my face, put water to my lips and let me have just a few sips. My "brothers" decided to go on without us, because they had to deliver the goods that same night.

When the sun began to set, the air became cooler. As I tried to get up, I threw up all the water the kind villagers had given me, but then I began to feel better. I tried to follow the caravan by crawling on my hands and knees, but Alam and I couldn't keep up the pace. They left us behind.

The camel owners went to the border and deposited the goods with the smugglers. They had papers to cross the border with camels, but not with merchandise. To our surprise, they waited for us. As the night air got fresher, I became stronger and before long, we came to where the caravan was waiting. We all crossed the border together.

Chapter VII

Once in Chad, Alam and I didn't know where to go. It was so dark I couldn't see a thing in front of me. Little by little I continued to regain my strength. Through the darkness I discerned the outline of an older man walking ahead of us, carrying heavy parcels. I suspected that each bundle was too weighty for me, but offered to help him anyhow, for I knew he would lead us to civilization. While Alam was clinging to one of my arms, clutching a couple of small bags of our clothing, I carried a bundle of the man's goods on the other arm and followed him towards the village. Suddenly, the piercing sound of barking dogs stopped me in my tracks. When I looked around, both the old man and Alam were gone. Afraid of being discovered by the hounds, I jumped over a small bush and hid breathlessly behind it, as still as possible, until the owner called the dogs home.

It was futile for me to go on by myself in the dark, so I stayed behind the bush until the sun came up. At dawn, the old man came looking for me, because I had some of his wares. I called to him and went out to greet him. He assured me that everything was all right. Alam was at his house and he invited me to come there, too. He was very hospitable, in the traditional way. He gave me food and water as soon as I got there, without asking any questions. He even provided us with a shower and had his daughter wash our clothes. We stayed with him for several days, while Alam and I had a good rest and became much stronger.

Our plan now was to go to the capital city to try to get some work – we didn't want to be stuck in that little village. We told our host that we were Muslims from Eritrea. He became all excited because he had a brother who fought in the Chad civil war and had a good friend in the Eritrean Liberation Front. He told us that because of the war in Chad, there were checkpoints everywhere. We needed to have a government-issued green citizen card, without which we couldn't get around. He offered to help us get it. His relative was the chief, and so, with a little bit of money, he was able to arrange it for us.

Chapter VIII

Equipped with green cards, we were ready to leave our new friend. He took us to a huge compound full of cars and trucks. We paid a truck driver to take us to Ambasha. We traveled all night until we came to another enormous compound in the city. There the officers checked everyone's papers. As I was carrying some of my family's pictures, I had no desire to be quizzed about who they were or where we were going. I told Alam to walk with me along the fence that goes from one side of the checkpoint to the other. To avoid arousing suspicion, we walked very nonchalantly, but when we came to the other exit, we bounded onto the other side.

Soon we came to a teahouse, where we stopped for a cup of tea and bread. The owner assumed we were Sudanese and was happy to say that he, too, was Sudanese. Wary of being discovered, I told him we were Eritrean, from a border town near Sudan. We became quite friendly and I asked him how much a bus ticket would cost us to go to the capital city. It turned out that we had just the exact amount of money left to buy two tickets. But, if we bought them, we would be penniless.

Alam and I began to quarrel. He didn't want to be broke. I felt very strongly that we had to get to the capital, or we'd never reach our final destination. I convinced him that we had no choice. I told him that if we reached the point where we had no food and were starving, we'd just have to beg. In the end he acquiesced and we purchased two rides, but were given no tickets; payment was apparently a somewhat informal affair.

We agreed to raise some money by selling a few of our belongings. I had a beautiful sweater and Alam had some expensive shirts, which could earn us a sizable sum. We returned to the teahouse and told the proprietor of our intentions. He helped us sell our garments, and when we asked if we might sleep in the teahouse overnight, he invited us to spend the night at his house and promised to get us to the depot on time next morning.

We graciously accepted his offer, and went home with him. We were surprised to see that he lived in a large compound with many relatives spanning several generations. The food they served us was no problem; Muslim dietary laws are quite similar to our own. However, in the midst of the settlement sat a beautiful mosque, and we were expected to go there and pray with the family. Both Alam, who was a Christian, and I, as a Jew, were forbidden by our religions to pray in a mosque. What should we do? If I were still in Ethiopia, I'd be severely punished for such a "crime." But I had learned when I was in Israel that the rabbis had declared that the precept of *pikuach nefesh* means that to save a life you may contravene existing biblical laws.

Neither of us had ever experienced the Muslim manner of praying. We were afraid our cover would be blown. Nevertheless, I decided that we should go along with our hosts to the mosque. I told Alam to observe what the others were doing and to copy their actions exactly. We washed our hands and feet, and then, while all the men were still standing upright in the assembly, we made our way to the back and imitated the actions of those in front of us. I silently prayed to the God of my Grandfather to forgive my transgression. Fortunately, we got by unnoticed; it was a matter of survival to break our traditional law.

Chapter IX

Early the following day, the teahouse owner's son took us to the terminal. There was a truck, not a bus, scheduled to leave for the capital. Although we had no tickets, the truck driver assured the ticket-taker that we had paid him and confessed that he had spent the money on beer.

We had to pass many checkpoints and were lucky to have our green cards. There was absolutely no trouble at all for us. We became friendly with the driver, who was very sociable. Along the way he noticed that we were penniless and that at times we begged for food. In typical Muslim hospitality, and sensitive to our condition, he bought food for us at every stop and invited us to eat with him as his guest.

After about a month of travel, we finally came to the capital city, Port Lamy, located on the Lamy River, which separates Chad from Cameroon. Its name was changed to Benjamina after the revolution. We were the only two passengers remaining on the truck. This, by coincidence, was where the driver, Omar, lived. When we got to our destination, Omar invited us to his house and asked his wife to prepare a snack for us. He then excused himself and explained that he had to go away for a little while to settle some transportation business.

Since Alam and I were smokers, we were dying for a cigarette, but had no money to buy them. We talked about our predicament and hit upon the idea of selling our *djellabas*; we didn't need them anymore, because the men there were dressed in French-style clothing. We washed them very carefully and dried them in about five minutes in the scorching heat.

The lady of the house directed us to the market along the only paved road in that town. As we neared the stalls, a man came up to me and said, "Hi, aren't you from Eritrea?" Believe it or not, we had a mutual acquaintance. He knew the tricks of the trade in that market and was able to sell the *djellabas* for us in no time at all.

With our newfound money, we bought cigarettes, soap for the house, and other small luxuries. A little later the driver came home carrying a box of beer, lots of food, and cigarettes. We had a great party that night. What a relief it was for us to let our guard down and enjoy ourselves.

Chapter x

That night I asked our host if he knew any Ethiopians, who might be able to help us "find our brother." He said he knew two people. I asked their names – I felt I could probably judge their ethnic origins by their names. One of them was Eritrean. I decided to stay away from that one, because we had lied about being Eritrean and it could backfire on us. The other was Hassan, an obvious Muslim name. I felt more secure talking to a Muslim from Ethiopia.

Our host offered to take us to Hassan's house. Just as we were approaching his home, we saw the Ethiopian in his Mercedes on his way to work. Our driver stopped him and announced that he had brought him two of his "brothers." Hassan was visibly shaken at the sight of these two wild men. Nevertheless he displayed customary Ethiopian hospitality and without asking any questions, invited us into his car and took us back to his villa, which was in a very large compound.

Hassan told his Libyan-born wife to bring us a refreshing drink and to give us fresh clothes. He led us to a beautiful big room and whispered more instructions to his wife. She provided us with pajamas, towels, and soap and showed us where the facilities were. Hassan said that he had to go back to work – he was the colonel in charge of military transportation in Chad, and people were waiting for him. Before long, his wife reappeared with a barber, who washed and cut our hair. We felt like we were in paradise.

When Hassan returned in the evening, there were still no questions asked. We were instructed, however, not to leave the compound. After about two weeks, when we were looking and feeling much better, Hassan, in one of our usual evenings together, told us that when he had first seen us, he was shocked at how bad we looked. He sensed there was something wrong. He felt that now that we were more relaxed, and knew and trusted him, we might be ready to tell him our story. We started to talk, but before we could tell him everything, he began to tell us his story.

Hassan explained that he had been born in Ethiopia and was originally a Christian. During World War II, when Italy had attacked Ethiopia (called Abyssinia then), Haile Selassie went to Jerusalem (which was under the British Mandate), then to England and to the League of Nations appealing for help. Britain sent General Wingate from Palestine to his aid, but his men could not prevail against the Italians. The emperor went to Sudan to gather some troops and tried to reenter his country via Sudan, but a group of men who had fought against the Italians and beat them back in their province, Gojam, did not let him come in. They felt he had betrayed his people when he left the country during their time of need and vowed never to let him reclaim the throne.

Haile Selassie, furious with these warriors, was determined to kill every last one of them. Balai Zeleke, Hassan's father, had been one of the rebel leaders and so the family's life was in danger. His mother, fearing for her son's safety, commissioned a Sudanese merchant to take Hassan with him to Sudan. There an Italian man adopted him and raised him as his own flesh and blood.

After Hassan had told us his story, I told him mine – that I had been educated in agriculture in Israel and was eager to find work. He asked, "Are you Falasha?" I told him the truth. He said that there were no jobs available in Chad. The only developed place in the whole country was the French military base; the rest was all desert. He advised us to go to Nigeria and offered to help us get there.

He suggested we go to the Nigerian embassy, say we were Eritrean, and ask for political asylum as refugees (because Eritrea was at war). We took his advice. He went out of his way to chauffeur us there, but, unfortunately, we were refused. They explained that because Nigeria had good relations with Ethiopia, and Eritrea was their enemy, they could not grant us refuge. I guess, politically, their friend's enemy was their enemy, too. There was nothing we could do about it.

Chapter XI

Hassan tried to find another way to assist us. He asked a trusted friend, whose business was the transportation of oil from Nigeria to Chad, to help us. The man agreed, but reminded us that first we had to get to Cameroon. The entry to Cameroon was across the bridge over the Lamy River, but we had no papers to pass through the checkpoint.

That night Hassan took us to the river. The three of us embarked in a canoe, which he had previously rented, and we paddled across the Lamy River to an isolated spot. He then hired a taxi and took us to a certain bar, where he told us we would be picked up by the oil tanker driver. Hassan gave us two hundred dollars each, one hundred to pay the driver and the other to pay for food. We parted with tears in our eyes, grateful for all he had done for us.

The driver arrived at the bar with his assistant and the four of us crowded into the cab of his tanker. He had to pay money at each checkpoint until we came to the Nigerian border. Of course we couldn't pass through, so we slept on the Cameroon side. Next morning, the driver sent his assistant to walk with me through the border. We had no trouble at all. The assistant returned and tried to bring Alam across, but the guards recognized him and told him that he had already brought someone across and sent them both back. I waited and waited in Nigeria and was beginning to lose hope of ever seeing Alam again. Nobody had told me that other arrangements had been made for my friend. At last I saw him coming through, escorted by another man. The driver had found someone else, who had agreed – for a certain fee – to bring Alam into Nigeria.

The driver and his assistant brought their vehicle into Nigeria (they had proper papers) and Alam and I piled into the cab with them, on our way to the capital, Lagos. It took us four days and nights of round-the-clock driving to get there. Pretty soon, we came to a big oil company, where my driver stopped to fill up his tanker. He told me that he wanted to do some shopping at a nearby company, but didn't know the language. I offered to work as his interpreter, for I had learned Arabic when my farm was on the Sudanese border (the language is close to Amharic and Hebrew). I suddenly saw this as an opportunity to earn a little money, as I was near the end of my allowance. I asked for a commission on the transactions, both from the seller and the buyer, who agreed to my proposal. At last I had a little spending money.

Lagos is a large city with over three million people, who are known for their intelligence and their industry. We stayed there for about a week, sleeping in the cab of the oil truck. Every day I went out to see if I could find work, but to no avail. On one occasion, I met a man who asked if I had come from Mecca and Medina. I said yes. He introduced me to his brother who was a Christian. I discovered that these men, like many others, were Christian one day and Muslim the other, depending on the situation. Before we parted, he amiably invited me to visit his beautiful mosque, and I accepted. I was gone longer than usual and Alam began to worry. By the time I got back he was very angry with me.

When our driver told us he had to return to Chad, we felt stranded. We needed a place to stay. While we were mulling over our options, the driver returned and said that he had promised to bring Hassan a letter in our handwriting, verifying that he had delivered us to Lagos. Otherwise, he (jokingly) said, Hassan would kill him. We happily gave it to him.

We asked neighbors where we might stay. As they didn't take kindly to strangers, they let us stay with them for only one night. At a teashop close by we inquired if we might stay at a nearby compound. They said we could try our luck. We went there, without realizing that this was an army camp. When the officer asked us who we were, I told him the truth. "Do you have passports?" he asked. "No," I replied. "Then," he warned, "you'd better leave before I call the police!"

Alam and I had no other choice but to sleep under a bridge. We got soaked from above by the rain and from below by the flooding. We were miserable. Alam got sick with a severe case of diarrhea. Both of us became weak and hungry. Finally I said, "I've had enough!" I practically carried Alam to a teahouse to have a hot drink and some bread. While sitting there, I saw a car with the name "Dizengoff Company" on it. I asked the driver if this was an Israeli company. He confirmed that it was and gave me the address: 24 Clark Street, in Appapa.

I told Alam that we had to be strong and that I must get to that company. I left him under the bridge and I walked and walked and walked until I found the office. I asked the receptionist to let me speak to the Israelis. She asked for my passport, but I had none. Since she wouldn't let me stay inside, I waited outside until I saw somebody about to go in. I stopped him and spoke to him in Hebrew. I asked him to please send the Israeli manager out to talk to me. He explained that he was only a visitor, but that he would try to do it. After about an hour, he came out and, when he saw me, struck his forehead and said, "I forgot!" I pleaded with him to give us some work, but he refused. He gave me five dollars and went away.

I got back to Alam before nightfall and told him that we had to find the Ethiopian Airlines office, where we could speak to an Ethiopian who might help us. We went back to the teahouse and asked the owner to kindly find the number of the Ethiopian Airlines for us in the telephone directory. He looked and looked, but was unable to find it. He did, however, locate the number of the

Ethiopian embassy, but it was futile for us to go there. We knew they wouldn't help, since we had escaped from their country.

Despondent, we returned to our "lodging" under the bridge. Just before we got to the bridge, however, we came across a garbage dump and I noticed a large sheet of yellow paper sticking out of it. Imagine our surprise when we found the name and address of the Ethiopian Airlines printed on it! It was 34 Breadfruit Street, a name that seemed to promise support.

We asked people where this street was and were told it was a long way off, too far to walk. Since we had no money to spare, we got up early next morning and trudged in the rain until we found the place, at about one o'clock in the afternoon. The office was closed. The sign said it would reopen at four. While we were waiting, dejected and exhausted, an Ethiopian-looking man (who was actually Sudanese) approached us and invited us to come out of the rain and rest at his home – just a block away – till the office reopened. He told us that he worked at a nearby Lebanese restaurant, and when we reached his house, he made us a salad and a delicious omelet. He then set about drying our clothes. We were so very thankful for his hospitality.

He took us back to the Ethiopian Airlines office where we told the secretary we wanted to see the manager. She went into his office, and we were delighted to hear that he had instructed her to send us in right away. When we came in, however, he was shocked to see us. He had been expecting some Ethiopian Airlines workers from England, who had an appointment with him at the same hour. Nevertheless, he asked us to sit down. I noticed from his nameplate that he was Eritrean, so I motioned to Alam to speak to him, because he was half Eritrean.

Alam told him our whole story. The manager found it hard to believe. He couldn't fathom how we had managed to cross through four countries (Sudan, Chad, Cameroon, and now Nigeria) without the necessary papers. In one way I couldn't blame him. At that time everybody was suspicious of everyone else – a man couldn't trust his own brother. Perhaps he feared we were government agents.

I described to him our living conditions under the bridge and the difficulties we were having. I asked if he could suggest some place where we might be given a little shelter. He was afraid to make a recommendation, but he put his hand in his pocket, gave us fifty dollars, and promised to see us again in a week. He gave us the name of an Italian friend who owned a construction company and suggested we ask him for a job.

I told Alam that I couldn't possibly go back to living under the bridge. I gave him the fifty dollars and said that, at this point, in spite of our pledge, we must part company. I advised him to go back to the Eritrean airline manager – "he is your brother" – and perhaps he would find a place for him. We hugged and said our goodbyes.

Chapter XII

made up my mind to go to the police station and tell them my story; I was not a criminal and I would fight for my rights. Out of the corner of my eye I saw Alam following me. He didn't want to be on his own.

When we reached the Lagos Central Police Station, I explained to the policeman all that we had gone through. He took the report and asked us to sign it, which we did, but it was a Friday and the chief was out of the office, not expected back until the following Monday. We would have to wait at the station until the chief returned. The policeman gave us a place to sleep in front of the door, but we were hungry and he wouldn't let us leave the premises. Finally, we begged him to let us go to a restaurant, accompanied by a guard. He agreed. When we sat down to eat, our escort insisted that we feed him, too. Fortunately we had the fifty dollars the Eritrean had given us.

On Saturday night, the police held a party in the compound; the chief came into the station and asked, "Where are the Ethiopians?" When he found us, he told us that, when he was studying in America, he had had an Ethiopian friend. Then he asked, "Do you have a passport?" Alam showed them his Ethiopian driver's license. He said, "OK, I'll see you on Monday." We thought that things would go well.

When the chief met with us on Monday, he didn't believe that we had come all the way from Ethiopia without documentation. He suspected that we were criminals who had burned our papers to avoid detection. He sent us to the Lion Building, a criminal investigation place; then he separated Alam from me and sent in three men to interrogate us individually. We told them the whole truth, but they still didn't believe us. They questioned us all day till late at night, without food or water. I was so weak and tired that I fainted in my chair. That's when the chief interrogator commanded us to be put in prison.

They locked us up in a cramped cell with about one hundred other men. It was horrible. There was no space to walk around. One tough guy was "the boss." He asked, "You come from Ethiopia? Are you a friend of Haile Selassie?" He was a great admirer of the Lion of Judah. I took out a picture of me standing with the watchman of one of the companies I used to work for, who looked just like the emperor. "The boss" was very impressed, and said that he, too, came from kings of an exalted Nigerian tribe.

In that jail, most of the inmates slept on the concrete floor. Only some "privileged" men slept on wooden pallets. "The boss" kicked one of them off his pallet and said, "You are nothing – this man is a king!" He offered the two-by-four to me, but I, in return, offered it to Alam because he was very weak. But he refused it. Alam, who couldn't stand the stench, the crowding, and the whole situation, stood up against the wall for three days and three nights until he collapsed. He was then taken to the infirmary, where he spent two weeks.

We were kept in that prison for six months. I had never before been in such a horrible place. You had to pay for everything, even for water. Sometimes they let us out into the yard to get a little exercise. Luckily, the cook, who supplied meals to the whole institution, took a liking to me. She asked the chief to let me come to the kitchen to assist her. Being there, I ate as much as I wanted and was even able to sneak some food out for Alam.

One day, "the boss" asked me why we were in prison. I told

him that we were not criminals, but, being related to Haile Selassie, who was an enemy of the revolution, we were seeking refugee status in Nigeria. He decided to help me. He asked, "Did you go to court?" When I told him that we never did have a court hearing, he outlined a plan for me. He said that the next time I was out exercising in the courtyard, I should hold back, kick up a rumpus and refuse to go back in.

The following day, I told Alam to stay with me while we were in the yard. When everyone paraded back in, I held onto the bars and started screaming, "I want to go to court!" The guards began beating my knuckles until they bled, but I didn't let go. The chief of police heard the commotion from the third floor and came running down into the courtyard. I shouted at him, "You are members of the United Nations and this is the way you treat refugees? We came here to save our lives and you treat us like criminals." He took us into his office, let us sleep on the benches, and agreed to get us a lawyer.

We waited two weeks for a lawyer. When he finally arrived, the police took us in chains to the courtroom. We waited our turn in an adjoining room, until we were summoned and placed on the platform. The judges asked us many questions. They wanted to know why, if we were legitimate refugees, we hadn't asked for asylum when we came to the border, before entering Nigeria. We told them that we had planned to go before a higher official, who would understand our situation better. They said, however, that once we had entered the country, we were there illegally and would have to be sent back to Ethiopia. Upon hearing this verdict, both Alam and I started to scream uncontrollably.

A lawyer, hearing our distress, came over to me and asked, "Are you Eritrean?" I understood what he was getting at (Eritrea was at war with Ethiopia and many people were seeking refugee status in 1974 and 1975), and I said yes. He said, "Now I understand." He went over to the judge and had a few words with him. I went over, too, and showed him some of my happy pictures. I explained that I didn't leave because I was hungry or out of work, but to save my life as a political refugee. He decided to send us to the minister of the interior in the immigration office, to review our case. They allowed us two weeks to try to straighten out our predicament.

Alam and I had agreed that, when questioned, I would always be Ethiopian and he would always be Eritrean, so that if one of us were given permission to stay, he should accept; and in all likelihood, we would not be forced to separate.

When we arrived at that department, we told our story to the chief, who happened to be a general. I told him – though it was not true – that the now well-known General Nega Tegegne (who was married to Haile Selassie's daughter) was my cousin and that I was one of the people who had tried to save him, but, afraid of being caught, I had run away. I relayed to him our whole story, the countries through which we had traveled and the terrible problems we were having. He said, "I'll see what I can do."

The general, however, couldn't do anything at that moment. He needed time to consult with the minister. In the meantime, he sent us to the Ikoyo police station – a more comfortable one – where we were free to move about, but only within the perimeters of the compound. Our appointment was supposed to be in two weeks. After one month, with nothing happening, I asked a policeman I had befriended if there was any way I could get out of that place. He said that the only hope I had was to go to the palace and lie down in front of the president and plead for my life.

Next day I jumped over the fence and followed the policeman to the gates of the presidential palace. I told the guard that I had come a long way to see President Yakuwu Gawan, who was a friend of "my cousin," Nega Tegegne. (This was actually true; I knew that Nega had worked with him at one time in Zaire.) The guard said that it was impossible to see him now; he was in England. I had to go back to the compound the way I had come. When I returned, I found Alam crying. He was terrified that he'd be beaten because I had escaped.

We were taken again to the immigration office. I judged the general's secretary, Ibrahim, to be Sudanese; he looked as though he came from the Sudanese and Chad border. He said that, yes, his origins were Sudanese. He looked more like we did, which made him more sympathetic to us, so we pleaded with him to help us. He took us to the general, who arranged to send us to a holding place at the airport, which was out of the city limits. We had a nice clean room, with lots of good food.

The secretary, Ibrahim, instructed us to call him in two weeks. He came and took us by Land Rover to the UN offices. He told them we were refugees accepted by the minister of the interior, but didn't have papers as yet; we needed assistance in the meantime. They gave us forms to fill out. Under "Languages" I wrote "Hebrew." They asked if I was related to Haile Selassie, the Lion of Judah. I replied that I had been selected by him to go to Israel to study Hebrew when I was young.

The UN people lodged us at the YMCA and gave us pocket money for food. At last we were free to move around. My roommate was an American who had come to Nigeria to buy African art. Not wanting to make waves, I told him that I was Christian. We became quite friendly and I accompanied him to the market to help him with the bargaining. By chance, I looked down at his insignia ring and noticed the Hebrew letter *mem*. I asked him if he was Jewish. He said, "Yes, my Hebrew name is Moshe." I told him I was Jewish, too, and then related to him the whole saga of our lengthy ordeal. He said, "Look, I'll take you to the American embassy. My mother is very active in the Jewish community in New York. Perhaps we can help." We tried that route, but, unfortunately, nothing came of it.

While we were stranded in the city and talking to others, we heard that Iraq was helping Eritrean refugees. Alam felt strongly that we should go to the Iraqi embassy and try our luck. When we got there, the ambassador became very angry and told us to go back to Eritrea. He asked, "Why did you come here to be a beggar instead of fighting for your country?" I told him, "You created the problem. You say you are a Muslim brother, but now that we are refugees and struggling, after our families and homes have been destroyed, you don't want to help us."

The ambassador became flustered and appointed someone else to take charge of our case. A rather quiet man took over. He said that if we really wanted to go to Iraq, we'd be required to do some army training there, but then we'd have to go back to Eritrea to fight for our country. We told him that we didn't come there to talk about fighting. We were desperate for food and needed help. He gave us some money and offered us twenty-five niras (the Nigerian currency) every week. He also gave us each a brochure to read about Iraq. These tracts were so vitriolic in their anti-Zionism, I couldn't believe my eyes. I saw red! I was so incensed, I burned my booklet. I told Alam that I would never go back to that embassy. If he wanted to go there to collect his money, he should go; but I would rather starve than take another penny from them. Again, Alam and I nearly parted company.

With friends after leaving prison in Lagos, Nigeria, 1975

Chapter XIII

I made up my mind to go back to the Dizengoff Company and see if they could find me work. I spoke to two Israelis there; regrettably, they could not hire me as I was not Nigerian and didn't have the right papers. They advised me to approach the (Israeli) Zim shipping company.

I spoke to the captain of one of their ships, telling him my whole story and pleading with him for work. But he remarked that I had been trained in agriculture – what did I know about sailing? I tried to convince him that I could learn to do anything; I needed work desperately and I was so anxious to get to Israel. He turned me down.

Feeling depressed, I wandered about the harbor, looking for someone to help me. Before long, I spotted a few Ethiopian sailors who, after I told them my troubles, gave me some money. Every day I went down to the wharf, looking for an opportunity to alleviate my situation.

A few days later, while sitting at a cafeteria on one of the ferries, I noticed a ship, called the *Gold Leaf*, anchored at the pier. But, under this heading, I made out, in faded paint, the Hebrew letters spelling the word "Haifa." I became energized. I ran over to the boat so quickly and scaled the ladder so fast that the watchman didn't have time to stop me. He yelled after me, "What are you doing?" He must have thought I was a thief. Just then, I spotted a white man on the top deck, who I assumed to be Israeli, and I shouted back to the watchman that I was going to see my friend. He stopped pursuing me. I asked him to please tell the man that I was waiting for him.

When the Israeli came down, he said, "What do you want?" I said, "*Shalom, adoni* (hello, sir)," and introduced myself. He in turn presented me to the captain. I told them my story and how much I wanted to go to Israel. The captain said that the ship was heading for Hong Kong the next day and couldn't take me on, because I didn't have a passport. I asked him, "If I did have a passport, would you take me?" "Yes," he replied.

My Israeli "friend," as I had called him to the watchman, worked on shore in a Zim company office. He gave me his card and invited me to come and see him whenever I wished. Feeling confused, I wandered back to Alam in a daze; it took me much longer to return from the ship than it had to go there.

Chapter XIV

At that time, in 1975, Nigeria was the biggest importer of cement in the whole world. Every day, there were around five hundred ships in the harbor waiting in line to unload their cargo, as the port was very small. I know of one ship that was there for over a year. The government of Nigeria footed the bill for all the delays. I used to help the men unload and sometimes they gave me tips, cigarettes, or other small gifts. That's how I managed to survive.

One day I asked a friendly sailor, who worked on a Greek ship, if it was possible for me to get a job with them. He said that his captain was away for a week and to come back then. I waited the week, then went on board and asked the captain if he would hire me. He asked, "Do you have a passport?" This time I said yes.

I went back to shore and racked my brain trying to figure out how to get a passport. I had heard that I could get a Nigerian passport for a hundred dollars, but I didn't have that much money. I decided instead to go to the Ethiopian embassy and try there. I filled out the application form, telling them what I thought they wanted to hear: I wrote that I had escaped during Haile Selassie's time in order to get an education, and that now I was determined to go back to serve under the people's government and to participate in building the new regime. I added that I had no passport and needed one to go back home.

I gave the form to the receptionist, who passed it on to the ambassador. I had known the ambassador for a very long time and was apprehensive as to how he would react. When I entered his office, I was relieved to see that he didn't recognize me. He asked me how on earth I had gotten into Nigeria. I told him that I had come all the way from Chad to get a passport, because there was no Ethiopian embassy in Chad. He couldn't believe that I had entered the country without papers. I explained that a good friend, who wanted to help me, had smuggled me in.

The ambassador asked, "So, you really want to go back to Ethiopia?" I said, "Yes, I really do." He told me that I didn't need a passport. All I needed was a *laissez-passer*. But I told him that I'd have to go back through Chad, Cameroon, and Sudan, and nobody would accept that slip of paper. I impressed upon him that I really needed to have a passport. He sighed and said, "All right. I'll arrange it for you. Do you have twenty-five dollars?" I was too close to my objective to let the lack of twenty-five dollars stop me now. I bluffed and said that I did.

I waited in the office and soon the receptionist told me that the passport was ready. She was prepared to give it to me, along with the prepared receipt, but I searched and searched my pockets, and, not surprisingly, couldn't find any money. I told her that I had forgotten my wallet at the hotel. I asked if she could give me the passport and I'd bring her the money the next day. Of course she refused and said she'd hold on to the document until I came back with the money. I had an impulse to grab the passport and run – it seemed to be my last chance. But I controlled myself and left the premises.

I thought and thought about how to get the twenty-five dollars. I couldn't find a way. Then I returned to the embassy and asked to speak to the ambassador once again. The secretary put me on the phone with him and he asked, "What do you want?"

Now, I had known the ambassador, Yftayi Demitrius, when I was at Kfar Batya in Israel. He was then a student at Hebrew University and after completing his education, he became the Ethiopian ambassador to Israel for ten years. I knew his whole family and he knew many members of my own. I explained that I had met him in Israel when he used to visit my ailing relative, Emmanuel Tamrat, and also another relation, Fitegu Tadesse. He was amazed. He said, "You're the little boy who was in Kfar Batya? You are so big now. Come, come right in."

I went back into the ambassador's office and told him my whole story – how I had lost my farm and the plight of my people, this time telling the unembellished truth. He said that he was familiar with the story, because his father, who was a patriarch in Ethiopia, and his brothers, who lived in Israel, had made him aware of the whole situation. He asked me why I hadn't told him the story before. I answered truthfully that it was because I was afraid. He offered to send a letter to the Israeli president, Chaim Herzog, to help me get to a kibbutz, but said we might have to wait a couple of months for a response. In the meantime, he gave me the passport, gratis, and told me to come back if I needed any kind of assistance. I was so very happy to get that passport.

To work on a ship, however, I needed not only a passport, but an inter-visa as well, for getting off the ship in the various ports. I called my old acquaintance, Ibrahim, at the Immigration Ministry, and told him that I had been offered a job on a ship, but needed both a passport and an inter-visa. I asked, "If I got a passport, would you be able to provide me with an inter-visa?" He said, "If you brought me your passport and a letter from the people who want to hire you, there'd be no problem."

I waited on shore for about a week for the Greek ship's captain. When he finally arrived, I greeted him warmly and reminded him of his employment offer. He cheerfully took me to the office of the Osanna shipping lines, typed out a letter, and handed it to me.

With the necessary documents in hand, I went off to see Ibrahim, who provided me with the official inter-visa. I made an appointment with the captain, who took me by boat to the ship, called *Apollonia Spirit*. I was now ready to set sail.

But I hadn't told Alam what I was doing. Alam had wanted to settle in one place. He was content that the United Nations had arranged and paid for him to go to high school. Because I didn't want him to be in a position to tell the authorities that I had escaped and so cause him problems, I reluctantly left him in Nigeria without saying goodbye.

Chapter XV

I had never worked as a sailor before in my whole life. My goal was to get to Israel and I intended to do whatever I had to do to in order to achieve it. The crew was diverse; the men came from Egypt, Nigeria, Pakistan, but most were from Greece. As I was not a professional sailor and didn't have insurance, they made me deck boy, assigned to swabbing floors and collecting and cleaning various tools. The captain, however, soon gave me real sailors' jobs to do – night watchman and other dangerous tasks.

The men cautioned me. They reminded me that I wasn't insured and if anything happened to me, I wouldn't be compensated. I confronted the captain. He said that if I wasn't happy, I should leave the ship. (We were still anchored near the port waiting to unload.)

I had befriended Ali, an Egyptian sailor – I spoke with him in Arabic – who asked me how much my pay slip was worth. When I showed him that it was three hundred dollars for two months, he got very angry. He said that he was paid five hundred dollars per month, and that the minimum I should have gotten as a deck boy, according to international law, was three hundred fifty dollars per month. I confronted the captain once again. He tried to appease me by saying that he had taken me on as a favor. I told him that he had cheated me and that I would not sign the pay slip, for if I did, it would indicate that I had accepted his allotment. I warned him that if he didn't give me my just pay, I would sue him when we landed. Again he threatened to leave me back on shore because of my insubordination.

This really made me angry. I took my bag of belongings and went into the kitchen, where I seized a butcher's cleaver. Then I returned to his office and told him that I was ready to go back to shore, but first he had to give me the seven hundred dollars he owed me. With that money I figured I could fly to Israel! He started in on me again and asked, "What do you know about the law?" I told him that all I wanted was my rightful pay, that I hadn't come there to be a slave and that he had a responsibility to pay me what I had earned. When he continued to object, I grabbed him by the neck and threatened him with the cleaver.

He began to yell and said he would call the police. I told him to go ahead and get the police for both of us. The chief officer, whose office was next door, heard the commotion, came in, and begged me not to make a mistake I would later regret. He bade me to quiet down and I suddenly remembered stories sailors had told me of how some captains threw Africans into the sea when they gave them trouble. I edged over to an open window and threw the cleaver into the water. I asked the CO if he was responsible for our pay and he said yes and assured me he would straighten things out.

Later he summoned me and explained that he had solved the problem. I was supposed to have signed a contract when I was hired, but never did. He drew up a contract in Greek and translated it for me. It was for one year from the day I started. Although the terms were very demanding on me, I didn't care. I signed it quite willingly, as my sole interest at that point was to get the money. I got my pay slips. In the meantime, the chief discovered that the captain had been stealing the difference between the money he was supposed to pay out and the amount he actually did disburse.

Chapter XVI

I stayed on the ship and worked, among other difficult jobs, as a watchman. I had to look out for pirates and other crafty thieves. Those were dangerous times. Every day we used to see dead bodies floating in the water.

I worked so hard that I developed seven big boils under my arm. I asked the captain to take me to a doctor, but he refused. He sadistically watched me from above to see if I was doing my job. To spite him, I'd stop what I was doing until he left. He got so mad that he came down and beat me, especially on my sores. I went screaming in pain to my cabin. Perhaps it was a blessing in disguise, because my boils burst.

Nevertheless, something in me snapped: I couldn't stand being abused and taken advantage of anymore. After all I had survived in my attempts to get to my homeland – the desert crossing, imprisonment, living under a bridge, and now this slavery to a brutal taskmaster – I just couldn't take any more assaults on my dignity. My anger welled up in me and I grabbed a hammer and went out on the ship looking for him. I spotted him talking to some workers. When he caught sight of me, he started to run. I chased him around and around the ship until I caught up to him and hit him in the back.

The chief officer leapt from his office and stopped me before

I could do more damage. He told me that, though he knew I was right and that the captain was crazy, he warned me to control myself; I was too emotional and could get myself into serious trouble and land in jail. He cautioned me once again not to take matters into my own hands and said that if I had any more problems, I should come to him. The men, on the other hand, were in awe at how I fought back.

The ship, after having lingered near Lagos for about a year, was finally permitted to enter the narrow port to discharge its cargo. Once we had unloaded everything, we were ready to sail. But the residue in the ship had to be cleaned out before we would be allowed to dock in the next port. It was hazardous, dusty work, wearing an uncomfortable mask, but it was also a chance to earn extra money.

The captain tried to force us all to clean each compartment for twenty dollars, whereas legally, the work was supposed to be voluntary and the pay one hundred dollars (to be shared among the sailors). The men, who were mostly foreigners and didn't understand the law, were prepared to accept. I refused. I explained to them their rightful dues and advised them to complain. They were afraid. I went alone to the captain and told him that we would agree to do the cleanup, but only if we got the one hundred dollars to which we were entitled. He asked me again, "What do you know about the law?" What I knew from bitter experience was that he wanted to keep the difference in the money for himself. I answered, "If you make anyone do it for less, I will kill you." I reported to the men what had transpired and they all agreed to reject his offer. We set sail without cleaning the ship.

Chapter XVII

The ship sailed from Lagos to Senegal, where we refueled in Dakar; then on to Casablanca, Morocco; and later to Majorca (off the coast of Spain). At that point I got very, very sick with either bronchitis or pneumonia; I had a high fever and couldn't breathe. From there we moved on to Greece.

When we landed, the captain went immediately to the police to lodge a complaint against me, telling them that I had threatened to kill him. Two policemen came to get me, but I informed them that I was not a Greek national and that they had no jurisdiction over me as long as I was on the ship. Furthermore, I accused the captain of treating me like a slave and added that I would report him to my embassy. The policemen left.

The chief officer saw how sick I was and took me to the hospital, where I spent twenty-three days. In the meantime he discovered how corrupt the captain had been and how much money he had stolen. Besides, he had docked the ship without having cleaned out the hold, which was supposed to have been done in the open sea, where it would not foul up the harbor. The company director was so infuriated, he fired the captain on the spot.

The ship was ready to leave while I was still lying in the hospital. The doctors couldn't seem to find the source of my illness. I had no money – just my pay slips – and no passport; it was being held on the ship. When I realized what was happening, I woke up. If I were to be stranded here without money or documents, I didn't know what would happen to me or how I would ever get to Israel. I made my way back to the ship and continued to work, even though I was very weak. The new captain told me that he had heard about me and treated me very nicely. Slowly, I started to feel better.

The ship sailed on to Port Said, Egypt. After we had landed, a mixed group of Egyptians made their way to the ship in small boats. Before long, it was transformed into a huge marketplace, with singing and dancing on a makeshift stage. There were all kinds of wares to be bought and the merchants spoke each sailor's language to him. I noticed that while the dancing was going on, some of the "guests" went off to the cabins to see what they could find for themselves.

Feeling rather tired, I went back to my cabin to rest. Soon one of the newcomers came into my room and asked me if I was Sudanese. I said yes. He told me that he had been in the war against Israel, that the Israelis had treated him very badly and that I should give him something, anything. I knew this lie was a ploy to get my sympathy, so I told him that I had nothing. He said, "Don't you even have a small pair of pants for me?" To get rid of him, I gave him an old pair of torn jeans, which seemed to satisfy him.

A while later, a couple of sailors knocked at my door and asked me to come and do some translating for them. They were negotiating to buy hashish from the Egyptians and didn't trust the foreign translators. The dealers gave the men samples to try, which put them in a very good mood, and they all agreed on a price. Several of the sailors didn't have money, so they traded cigarettes from the ship's stock in exchange for the drugs.

Days later, after we had left the Suez Canal and were out in the open sea (where there were no authorities to stop them), the men tried to smoke the stuff, but it wouldn't burn. Evidently, what they were sold wasn't real hashish. The men were furious because they had lost so much money. They redirected their anger to me and accused me of not telling them the truth. I had to work very hard to convince them that I was just an innocent bystander and had nothing to do with the whole transaction. All I did was translate, as they had asked me to do. At that time, I didn't even know what hashish was supposed to look like.

Chapter XVIII

E ach ship had to stay in line to cross the Suez Canal. While we were waiting our turn, I kept looking out the window and toying with thoughts of jumping into the water and swimming to Israel. But the distance was too far and my health too poor.

It took us four days to sail from Suez to Singapore, which has the largest facility in the world for repairing boats. There we spent time in dry dock, repairing our ship. We had to get it into shape before moving on to Sydney, Australia, to pick up a large cargo of meat. We were all busy, cleaning, painting, fixing; I was on a tall ladder, tightening a bolt with a wrench, when I fell down ten feet and fainted. My back was broken in the fall. I was rushed by ambulance to a hospital, where they kept me in a "dead sleep" for a whole month in order to keep me rigid, without moving a muscle.

One day, I heard the man in the next bed say that the Israelis had captured the whole of Africa and were now going to take over the rest of the world. Too ill to question him, I remained silent. I later found out that what he had heard was how Israeli commandos flew four thousand kilometers (2500 miles) and raided the Entebbe Airport (July 4, 1976) to rescue one hundred five of their compatriots who had been hijacked on an Air France plane, diverted from its course to Athens and landed in Entebbe, Uganda. How the myth of the "Jewish conspiracy" to rule the world has entered the psyche of so many people! The fact, however, that Israel was willing and able to reach out to Africa to save its own people gave me a deep feeling of pride and reinforced my hope that one day my Ethiopian brothers and sisters would be rescued as well.

Meanwhile, the ship had been repaired and was set to sail. The captain and the company's agent came to visit me and told me that if I were well I should come back to the ship as soon as possible. But if the doctor said that I needed more time to recuperate, then I could probably get work on another one of their ships at a later date. If not, they offered to fly me to their next destination in Australia. My life was now in the hands of the agent. The doctor sent the whole report to him, where it stated clearly that I was very ill and I must not work for at least another four months.

The medical staff, which included a social worker, advised me to go home to my family in Ethiopia, to get the tender loving care I needed. They all tried hard to persuade me to do that. At that point, I confessed to the doctor that I was a refugee and couldn't possibly go home. I pleaded with him to say that I was well, but he said he couldn't do that, because he had already handed in his report and couldn't make any changes now. Besides, he reminded me that I was not well enough to work anywhere and needed to have a long rest.

I asked the agent to give me the money he owed me and to return my passport. I thought I'd get a visa to go to Israel. But they insisted that I go back to Ethiopia. I had read, however, that a sailor in my circumstances had to be sent back to the place where the ship originated, which for me was Nigeria. They gave me my money and my passport, but it had expired.

Now, after all my troubles at sea, and once again with problematic papers, I had to make my way back to Nigeria.

Chapter XIX

agonized over what to do. I hated the idea of breaking the law, but I rationalized to myself that the whole immigration system was just a bureaucracy. The expiration date on my passport was 1975; I carefully changed the number from a 5 to a 6. When my health started to improve, I bought a ticket to fly via Singapore Airlines from Singapore to Bombay, India; then by East African Airlines to Karachi, Pakistan; onward to Dubai in the United Arab Emirates; and then to Kenya. In the duty-free shop I bought a stereo, several watches, and other merchandise that I planned to sell later in order to make some money.

In Kenya I went off to see if I could find the Israeli embassy, but was told they had none and all their dealings were done through the Swedish embassy. I had no time to go there; I had to catch my flight with Pan American Airlines, which went to Zaire and then to Nigeria. I was asked to pay airport taxes for all the merchandise I had bought. I told them I had no money. The official kicked up a commotion and sent me to the customs office, but I went to the washroom instead and came back just in time to get onto the plane. I hurriedly gave him a bribe of twenty-five shillings and he let me board.

When I arrived in Nigeria, the immigration officer didn't want to let me in. Although I had a passport, I didn't have an entry visa. I explained that I was a sailor, just passing through to get to my ship. I gave him the ship's name and that of the agent. Then I handed him ten dollars and he gave me a forty-eight-hour pass, after which I had to be out of the country.

I made my way to the YMCA, at 77 Awolowolo Road, and waited for Alam. We were both so excited to see each other. I related to him my whole story. He told me that the UN refugee commission had given him a rough time trying to find out where I was. They couldn't believe that he really didn't know what happened to me.

Alam updated me on his present activities and said that he was quite happy with his choice of courses at school. I visited with other friends, as well, and caught up on all the gossip.

During the next few days, disregarding the orders the doctor in Singapore had given me, I tried to find work. I went to the Zim office and they told me to come back in four months. I wandered around the harbor looking for another ship – now that I was an experienced sailor – but couldn't find anything that would bring me closer to my goal.

Although I had a little money, I didn't want to spend it all, so I did some business on shore, participating in some deals with the sailors. They were very friendly and often treated me to lunch.

One day, while having a snack on a ferry, I overheard a couple of sailors on the other side of the bar speaking Hebrew. I went over to them and greeted them in their language. They were surprised and asked: "Are you from Ethiopia? Are you Falasha?" We got into an animated conversation and I explained to them my predicament. They thought that the best thing for me to do was to get to Israel and work there on a kibbutz. But I didn't have an Israeli visa. They advised me to go straight to Israel and explain everything to the immigration department once I got there. They encouraged me that I would find there the acceptance that had been avoiding me so far. "They will understand."

Chapter xx

As soon as I could, I went over to an Alitalia office and found that for six hundred dollars I could buy a one-way ticket from Lagos to Israel, with a stopover in Rome. Although they didn't ask for it, I thought it best to have an Italian visa, in case, for some reason or other, I was delayed in Rome. An Eritrean friend, who knew the Eritrean secretary at the Italian embassy, accompanied me there and helped me fill out an application form.

The visa arrived fifteen days later. I rushed off to the airport at the appropriate time and bought my ticket. The immigration officer looked at my passport and sternly took note of the fact that I had a forty-eight-hour pass to be in Lagos, and here it was several weeks later. I told him that I had been very sick, that I had suffered from severe stomach troubles and that good friends had looked after me. I begged him to let me go, because I had relatives waiting for me in Rome. I showed him my Italian visa. He kept me waiting while everyone else boarded the plane. I was left all alone and didn't know what was going to happen. Finally, he gave me an exit stamp and cautioned, "Don't ever do this again."

At last I was on my way. A white man sat beside me. We had very little to say to each other, but soon, a little girl who was seated across the aisle beside us ran over to him and exclaimed, "*Abba,*

Abba!" "Ah," I said, "You must be going to Israel, too!" From then on we became friendly and I learned that he worked for a large construction company in Nigeria and that he and his family were going to spend their vacation in Israel.

When we landed in Rome, the Israeli man, his family, and I went over to El Al Airlines. They passed through without a hitch, but I was held back; I didn't have an Israeli visa! I spoke to them in Hebrew and told them my story, but it didn't help. The man I had befriended came back and tried to defend me, but to no avail. The Israeli guard suggested I go back to the Alitalia office. At Alitalia they said I should have gotten the visa in Nigeria, before I had taken the flight. At this point, they advised me that the only solution was to go back to Nigeria.

I got very angry and asked them why they hadn't told me that in Nigeria when I bought my ticket to Israel. I said, in no uncertain terms, that I would not go back. I made it quite clear that it was *their* mistake and that *they* had to fix it. After a brief consultation, they decided to let me stay one night in Rome to try to get an Israeli visa from the Israeli embassy the next day. They put me up in a beautiful room at the Holiday Inn, meals included.

I couldn't sleep all night, I was so excited to go to Israel. I got up early the next morning and went by taxi to the Israeli embassy. It was much too early and the gate was closed. The security was tight. I told the guard in Hebrew that I wanted to go to the land of my forefathers; I needed to get into to the embassy to get a visa in order to fulfill my dreams. He told me to come back at nine o'clock when the offices opened.

I crossed the street and stayed there until I saw the gate unlocked. Once inside the courtyard, I waited my turn in a large area outside the building. At last I was summoned. I told the man my story and presented my papers. The verdict was: no visa. The agent said I needed five hundred dollars and a three-month return ticket to Italy. "Look," I told him, "I'm not a tourist. I want to make *aliyah*; I want to go back home to Israel." He refused.

I was very upset, and all the emotion of my endless journey

poured out. I told him: "When we were in Ethiopia, though we were the same color as the others, they treated us badly because we were Jews. Now that I want to go to Israel, to live with my fellow Jews, you deny me a visa because I am black. When six million Jews were slaughtered in Europe, they were exterminated because they were Jewish; nobody looked at their color. This is what we are facing in Ethiopia. I will stay here until I get my visa, or you will have to carry my dead body out of here."

The agent seemed sympathetic, and he relented, saying, "Let me try again." He went to the secretary's office and asked her to come out and assist in my case. She spoke to me in English, but I appealed to her in Hebrew; I told her that I had spent almost ten years in Israel, was educated there, and now I wanted to go back to live there. She said she was very sorry, but she couldn't do anything right now, because the ambassador was away. I asked her how come some of the people with whom I had traveled were able to get visas while the ambassador was away. She said that these visas were prearranged. I told her that I couldn't go anywhere else, that Israel was the only place for me. I asked her, "Where do you think I should go – do you want me to go to the moon?" She said, "Oh, you mean you want to make *aliyah?* We don't deal with that here. You will have to go to the Jewish Agency for that."

I took a taxi and went straight there.

Chapter XXI

At the Jewish Agency, everybody had to put their documents through a slot, while they were watched by closed circuit TV. While sitting in the waiting room, I looked into the office and thought I recognized one of the men. Finally my turn came up and when I went into the office, the man asked me if I was from Ethiopia. He remarked that he had lived in Ethiopia, too. Then I recognized him as Naphtali Bar-Shalom, who had been the military adviser to Haile Selassie; I had met him and his wife when I was working at the Amiran Company – his wife and my boss's wife were very good friends and they'd often come down to the office together. After I had refreshed his memory, he said to me, "Are you Baruch?" He became so excited, he phoned his wife to come to his office immediately – he had a surprise for her. When she saw me, she shrieked with joy and threw her arms around me. It had been a long time since I was made to feel so welcomed and protected.

They were most anxious to hear my story, so Naphtali closed the office door to ensure our privacy and we talked for three hours. They found it unbelievable how I had managed to get there after all I had been through. When he discovered that I had only forty dollars to my name, he put me up in a kosher hotel run by a woman named Miriam Bachbut, at his expense, and provided a driver for me while he was scheduled to be in Milan for the next two weeks.

As I stretched out on the hotel bed, I gradually started to feel the inner tension and heavy pressure lift from my tortured soul. I slept day and night for I don't know how long, while the driver waited patiently for me. At last he saw me emerge from my stupor. He took me to see all the synagogues in Rome and gave me guided tours around the city. As instructed, he looked after all my needs.

Finally, Naphtali Bar-Shalom came back and gave me the bitter news: the Jewish Agency had denied my application for *aliyah*. He couldn't explain their incompetence, but said, "Don't worry; I am a good friend of Uzi Narkis, head of the Jewish Agency in Israel." He phoned him and Narkis instructed him to put me on the plane. Then he wrote a letter for me to give the El Al clerk at the airport. He assured me, "You will have no problems."

At the airport I presented the letter to the agent, and again was kept waiting. Many Russian and other immigrants had boarded the plane and I was left to myself. What now? I braced myself for the worst. At last a stewardess came to get me. She presented me with a bouquet of flowers and led me to the airplane, where the officers and crew were lined up along the aisle to greet me as an honored guest. Each one shook my hand, saying, "*Kol hakavod, Kol hakavod!* (Congratulations, kudos to you!)" I couldn't imagine what Naphtali Bar-Shalom had written in the letter, but I was thrilled by their welcome.

We landed at Lod Airport in the evening. It had taken two years and eight months of painful wandering from the time I had left war-ravaged Ethiopia until my arrival in Israel. For the second time in my life I lay down and kissed the holy soil. Again, I thanked the God of my Grandfather for delivering me to the Promised Land. I was so ecstatic to have finally reached my destination.

Chapter XXII

My elation, however, was short-lived. After having passed through security, I was taken to the *aliyah* office, where they processed immigrants who were planning to settle in Israel. People were called into the office one by one, but they never called my name. It was close to midnight and I was the only one left in the waiting room. I knocked at the door and said, "*Adoni* (Sir), what about me?"

He told me that the Ethiopians have to be processed not only through the *aliyah* office, but also the Ministry of Religious Affairs, the Ministry of Foreign Affairs, and a couple of other ministries, all closed at that hour. I asked him, in Hebrew, "How come all the others got their papers and I am the only one not accepted? I gave you all my documents; everything is in order. Why do I have to go through all the other ministries?"

He replied, "You have to spend the night here and we will make the necessary arrangements in the morning."

At that point my blood was beginning to boil. I said, "I gave you my papers – is there anything wrong with me? If so, tell me. According to the Law of Return, you are supposed to admit every Jew who wants to "return home" unless he has a criminal record. Am I a criminal? I saw many others go through – some of the Russians don't even look Jewish, yet they had no problems. None of the others spoke Hebrew; I'm the only one who knows the language. Why are you stopping me? Is it because of my color?" He said, "Don't shout at me!" When he said that, I reached a point of desperation and grabbed him by the neck. I cried out, "Show me where the door is. Either you let me into Israel tonight, or you send me back to Italy. I had enough enemies in Ethiopia; I don't need a brother as an enemy." He started to scream. We made so much noise that the police and the other workers barged in.

After nearly three years of hiding, running, imprisonment, and enslavement, I had finally reached my treasured homeland, and now the police were coming to arrest me! I offered the police, in Hebrew, my impassioned plea: "I have come all the way to Israel to seek refuge from Ethiopian oppression. My people have suffered for thousands of years to maintain our religion. We were always sustained by the hope of returning to Jerusalem. My papers are in order and this bureaucrat is not letting me enter. If you don't want blacks here, you should put up a big sign saying 'NO BLACKS ALLOWED.'"

I was so distressed and offended, I started to cry in front of everybody. A sympathetic elderly woman came over and tried to comfort me. Devastated, I fell to the ground.

When things cooled down a little, the agent took me to a hotel to spend the night. There I bumped into some of the other immigrants I had met at the *aliyah* office. They were to be transferred the next day to various absorption centers.

When I lay down on my bed, I was inconsolable. I was so humiliated that tears still well up in my eyes whenever I think about that night. How could they treat me this way? I waited a whole week and nobody called. To add insult to injury, the hotel manager presented me with a bill for the week's lodging. I explained that I had been sent there by the Jewish Agency at their expense. He told me they had paid for only one night; the rest was my responsibility. I stubbornly refused. He called the Jewish Agency and they agreed to foot the bill. They added that I should go to my relatives, whose names I had written on my application, and join them on their kibbutz. I took the phone and asked, "Do you do this for every immigrant? Why don't you treat me like everyone else? You still have a problem recognizing the authenticity of Ethiopian Jews. I demand my rights as a Jew. If you have a problem with the color black, then take the black spots out of the middle of your eyes."

The agent mellowed and said, "All right, take a taxi and come back here to the airport." When I finally got there, at long last, he gave me my immigrant card along with some spending money and arranged for me to go to an absorption center in Herzliya.*

Absorption Center, Atlit, Israel, 1986

---

* For map of itinerary see appendix 1.

SECTION 3
The Promised Land

Chapter 1

I began my adult life in Herzliya, Israel, in August, 1976, when I was thirty-two years old. I was looking forward to settling down, getting married, having a family, and starting a new life. Naphtali Bar-Shalom had given me the telephone numbers of a few people I had known in Ethiopia, who were then living in Israel. I called David Ram, of the Ethiopian Amiran Company, and asked if he knew where I might get work. He was very happy to hear from me and recommended me to Yitzhak Kirnitsky, a manufacturer of agricultural machinery who was represented by the Koor Company. I was hired on the spot. One job, however, wasn't enough for me, so I took on another as night watchman in a hotel, in order to put away money for the future.

At the Koor Company, because of my experience in the field I was put in charge of a department that assembled machinery parts. Others who had been there much longer were jealous and began insulting and taunting me. I remained calm and patient and went about my duties, trying to ignore their remarks. After a while, my section started to produce more than twice as much as it used to. The men resented my efforts and called me *chamor* (donkey, or boss's toady).

One afternoon, while I was working under a machine, covered in grease, one of the workers who always mocked me came over and began hurling insults at me. He laughed and said, "You're dirty to begin with and now you're even dirtier." That was the last straw. I pushed the heavy machine away from me – I don't know where I got the strength – then pulled myself up and chased after him. The boss came over and tried to stop me, but in my rage I threw him down and went home. I stayed in my room for three days and couldn't eat a thing.

I just kept trying to understand: Why?

Sarah, the hostel counselor, came knocking at my door and told me that Mr. Kirnitsky was looking for me. She was visibly alarmed to see my condition and asked, "What happened to you?" I'm afraid I wasn't too communicative. She insisted I come down to the office and return the phone call. When I called the factory they told me that the owner was not available. The next day, Mr. Kirnitsky appeared at my door. He convinced me that it was imperative for me to go back to work, that I must be strong and not be intimidated by stupid people. He had fired my tormentor and assured me that no one would ever harm me again. He added that he had convened a meeting with all the employees and threatened to fire anyone who showed the least bit of racial prejudice.

Mr. Kirnitsky transferred me to a new place and put me to work with several mechanical engineers. He made me head of the shipping department. I was to look after all the details, like packaging, weighing, routing, etc. Sometimes there was a big rush to get the machinery out on time and I often had to work late into the evening. I had no objection, because I knew how that business operated. One day, when I asked a new Arab employee to work a little faster because a shipment was due, he said, "*Cushi*, don't tell me what to do."

My temper reappeared in full force. I grabbed him by the neck and pushed him into a garbage pail. I realized then and there that I couldn't educate five million people; it was too much for me. My supervisor came and told me to control myself; he said that I should come to him if I had any more problems. I replied, "I'm a man and I have to defend myself." The whole episode was too much for me. I quit my job and left.

Chapter 11

There were all kinds of immigrants at the hostel; from Russia, Morocco, South America, the USA, Canada, etc. I was the only black there. The manager looked down his nose at all of us, but was especially mean to me. He once said, "We have enough barbarians here; why did they send me someone from the trees of the jungle?"

Because I spoke Hebrew, I was one of the people delegated by the others to bring our complaints to the manager. On one occasion I was asked to speak to him about our isolation. I explained that we were all immigrants, and though we were very happy to be in Israel, we weren't familiar with the country. (I had of course lived in Israel when I was younger, but I had never had an opportunity to see much of the land.) We wanted to know if he could possibly arrange for a tour to introduce us to our surroundings. We were also interested in making connections with other Israelis, learning Israeli folk dances, songs, etc. His response was, "What do you know? You don't know anything." This man was the bane of my existence.

At that time, we were all young and most of us had paired up with boyfriends or girlfriends. I had met a lovely (white) English girl and we started to date. The manager wrote to the head of the Jewish Agency stating that I was consorting with a Jewish woman and that something should be done to stop me, because she was Jewish and I wasn't. He said I had done something against the Jewish religion that had tainted not only the hostel, but the whole neighborhood as well. He claimed, too, that all the friends who came to visit me were criminals and demanded that the Agency remove me from the hostel as soon as possible. The Agency person agreed that, for both our sakes, I should move. In spite of the fact that there was a four-year waiting list for the other place, they were prepared to put me at the head of the line and move me in right away. But I said, "No, it's not fair to those who have been waiting all this time to go there."

When I found out what the manager had written in his letter, I was furious. I asked him, "What did I do against the Jewish religion?" He said, "You were sleeping with a woman without being married to her." "But," I objected, "practically everyone here has someone else in their bed – why are you picking on me?" He gave me a dirty look.

Failing at his attempt to get me out, the manager started to harass me. He called the police and told them that I had criminal friends who came to the house regularly and that it was dangerous for the whole area. I asked the officer, "If they are criminals, why don't you put them in jail?" The policeman seemed to size up the situation, looked straight at me and said, "Sorry," and went away.

A few months later my girlfriend revealed to me that she was pregnant. I was terribly confused. Although I really liked her very much and would have loved to have had a child, I was in no position to raise and support a family. I went to David Ram from Amiran to ask his advice. He suggested that we move to a kibbutz, where we would have no financial problems. But my girlfriend didn't like that idea at all; she was not partial to collective living. She called her sister who came from England to see her and, together, they decided on an abortion.

Chapter III

We young people often went to the beach, played our guitars, and sang around the bonfire, while others roasted potatoes. One balmy evening, the police came along to see what was going on. Four of them walked over to me and asked for my identity papers. My back went up. "Why," I asked, "out of all the two hundred fifty people here do you come straight to me? Do I look like a Nazi? If you are going to check identity papers, check everybody's, not just mine." One of them told me not to be so impudent. I retorted, "You are a man. If you want my identity papers, you'll have to take them from me; I'm not going to give them to you."

Lou, a friend of mine, who was originally from Ireland, heard me arguing and came over to see what was happening. When he learned what the police were doing, he lost his temper and began to rant and rave. Many others joined in the commotion and, to calm things down, the police backed off. Next day, to his credit, the policeman appeared at my door and apologized for his actions. He said that I had taught him something he would never forget.

Every day I encountered some signs of prejudice. I couldn't understand how people who were supposed to be my brothers could behave so poorly. I corrected them some of the time, but most of the time I was patient and even went so far as to make a joke of it. When people asked me where I came from, I'd answer, "Sweden." Sometimes you can teach best through humor.

Chapter IV

I was looking for a job and noticed in the paper an advertisement for "roughnecks." I didn't know what it was all about, but the pay looked good, so I applied. The agent thought I was experienced, and hired me.

The job entailed working for Ramco, an English oil drilling company, in the south, near El Arish. From there we flew by helicopter to a boat in the Mediterranean Sea. When we disembarked, I sat beside an Englishman who asked me what my post was and I told him, "roughneck." I asked him what he did on the ship and he said he was my boss. Then he asked if I knew what a roughneck was. "No," I replied. "Don't worry," he said, "the men will teach you all about it."

They began to train me. I had never realized how difficult that job was. Four men had to turn and guide a very long and heavy nine-ton pipe, which was attached to a compressor that was part of the oil drill. I worked with an Englishman, a Texan, and a German. We had to work as a team and look after each other; one false move and somebody could get killed. At first, I didn't know how to synchronize my timing with the others. They started to curse me and called me all kinds of vile names. The manager came over, took my place, and instructed me to watch carefully. He demonstrated what I needed to do. After that I was able to do my job pretty well and before long I was a real pro. We worked twelve-hour days for two weeks at a time. After the first two-week shift, they posted a list of who should come back and who shouldn't. I was worried about my chances, but was happy to see my name on the "come back" list.

After having worked for eight months on the rig, I had an accident. The sea was particularly rough when it was my turn to pass the pipe on to my replacement. For some reason he didn't take into account the violent movement of the waves, so he lost his balance and couldn't grab onto the greasy cylinder. The heavy force of the swaying pipe threw him aside and then hit me across my shoulders. I passed out.

The company helicopter was unavailable at that time, so the manager called the Israeli military for help. They sent a helicopter and I was airlifted to the roof of a hospital in Beersheba. The staff, thinking I was a Bedouin fedayeen who had been shot by the military for some misdemeanor, left me waiting until they attended to other priorities. I started to scream and yell for attention. They finally put me into a bed, unwashed and still covered in grease. Next day they gave me a shower and took me upstairs for x-rays. The technician evidently didn't realize I understood the language, as she made no attempt to modify her voice when she phoned down to ask, "Why did you send me an Arab?" I took a deep breath and scolded, "Your job is to cure people, regardless of their color." She turned red and apologized.

I was unable to work for four months. Fortunately the company's insurance policy compensated me for that time. Although my job was waiting for me, I decided to use the money I had earned to go into business for myself. A Yemenite man I knew (born in Ethiopia) owned a delicatessen near my hostel and was looking for a partner. We signed an agreement and I began to work with him. We got along very well.

Chapter v

At that time, in 1977, there were about two hundred fifty
Ethiopian Jews living in Israel, none of whom had come
on *aliyah*, as permanent immigrants. They were there to
fulfill specific job contracts or had escaped to Eilat by boat and
then made their way up north. They had no status as Israeli citizens,
because there was confusion as to their identity as Jews under the
Law of Return, and they were therefore constantly threatened with
deportation.

Previously, an Ethiopian native, Hezi Ovadia, son of Yemenite parents, after having retired as top sergeant in the Israeli army,
had decided to devote all his energies to helping his people both
in Israel and back home. He wrote a letter to the Sephardi chief
rabbi, Ovadia Yosef, requesting an official document verifying our
Jewishness. In 1973, Rabbi Yosef issued that vital confirmation. His
landmark decision made a big difference in people's attitudes to
Ethiopian Jews. The rabbinate, however, insisted on a symbolic
conversion, without which the Bet Yisrael members would not
be recognized as authentic Jews; which means that they could receive only permanent residence status, not citizenship. Then, in
1975, the Ashkenazi chief rabbi, Shlomo Goren, went along with
his colleague's ruling. He co-affirmed the Jewishness of Bet Yisrael
and welcomed their immigration and absorption.

The government, however, was reluctant to accept the Bet Yisrael as Jews. They were still not able to enter Israel as citizens under the Law of Return. It was even forbidden to talk about their plight in public. Hezi gathered together some of the Ethiopian Jews who were in Israel – from those who worked in chemical plants near the Dead Sea to those further north who were there on various contracts – and lobbied the government for changes to their status.

Hezi had heard about me and visited me when I first arrived in Herzliya. He wanted to hear my whole story, and when he did, he insisted I write it all down. We used to meet regularly at the Faitlovitch House, and he became more and more involved in our cause. At a later date he even went to Kenya to help in a rescue mission.

One evening, an Israeli, Eli Turgeman, who had been working for the Jewish education and training organization ORT in Ethiopia for two years, brought us a letter from the Jewish community that said, "Save us! Save our children! Please tell the Israeli government to do something!" One story in particular moved me to the core. It was about a woman and her child who were sold into slavery. Our people were suffering terribly. This was happening because there were two Ethiopian groups vying for power – the government and the opposition – and the Jews were caught in the middle. They were in a "no win" situation; if they chose the government, the others would kill them; if they sided with the opposition, then the government would imprison them.

Mr. Turgeman told us that he had gone to the Israeli government for help, but they didn't want to hear about it. He insisted that it was up to us to get them to listen. When I read the letter for myself – it was in Hebrew – I became terribly disturbed. I felt moved and obligated to do something. I stood up and said, "As the Ethiopian saying goes, 'if the baby doesn't cry, it will never get milk.' We have to do whatever is in our power to make ourselves heard. If we remain silent, nothing will be done. We have to learn from the Russians and make demonstrations."

My people were used to keeping a low profile and didn't want to stir things up. Some said, "Be patient, the Israeli government will help us, don't worry." I countered, "Israel has existed for thirty years and still hasn't done anything for us. If we want our families to come to Israel, we have to lobby and make ourselves heard. There are many Israelis, inside and outside the government, who will support us. Let's have a demonstration!"

Most of those present agreed and we formed a committee to organize a protest. We set a date and got a license from the police. We elected two men, Zimma Barhanu and Zecharia Yona, to be in charge. I hired a bus – which I paid for myself – to collect all our people to go to Jerusalem. The evening before the appointed day, we had a general meeting to finalize plans – where to meet the bus, what clothes to wear (it was cold in Jerusalem), what food to bring, etc. At that meeting, our two chairmen stopped the proceedings to read a telegram they had received from Prime Minister Begin, which stated, "Please don't make any demonstrations."

I stood up and said, "Your father, your mother, your family are suffering in Ethiopia. If you don't care about them, if you always listen when people say, 'don't do this, don't say that,' you will never be able to help them. In the end we will be responsible for these people dying in Ethiopia. Any one of you who wants to bring his family out of Ethiopia, and is not afraid, come with me." Some people left, but ninety stayed and agreed to join me in the demonstration. Later that evening, I happened to mention what happened at the meeting to an Israeli friend. He said that his brother lived in a group home in Jaffa and if I provided them with a bus and some sandwiches, they'd surely go along. We arranged for transportation and food and they happily joined us.

When Begin saw the demonstration outside his window, he noticed the number of white Israelis who mingled with the black. This, apparently, left a lasting impression on him.

My fellow Ethiopians were too shy to clamor for attention, but I, having been brought up in democratic Israel, knew my rights and had the self-confidence to make myself heard. I chained myself to the gate, *took off my clothes*, and quoted from the Song of Songs (1:5–6): "I am black and comely…Look not upon me because

I am black…" I asked, "Is it a crime to be black and Jewish?" The newspapers and television covered the event, giving it tremendous publicity. From then on, whenever I walked in the street, people stopped and asked, "Are you from Ethiopia?" The public became more aware of our situation and grew more supportive of our demands. They had never before recognized the difference between us and the black Americans or the dark Bedouins.

That demonstration made a great difference. Begin agreed to meet with us. He said he couldn't do anything just then, because Israel didn't have diplomatic relations with Ethiopia. He said he understood the dire predicament of the Ethiopian Jews, but couldn't see a way out at that particular time. But he promised to try to do something.

Chapter VI

Meanwhile, I was called up to serve in the Israel Defense Forces (IDF). With my partner's blessings, I went off to join the army, with the understanding that I'd work at the store whenever I had time off.

After I passed my medical, I asked my superior, "Why do I have to serve in the army? I don't have any family here." Naively, I had hoped that the government would be honor-bound to bring my family to Israel, but my ploy didn't work. Before starting training, they sent me along with some of the other recruits to an *ulpan* to learn Hebrew. I didn't participate very much in class; nevertheless, I placed first in the exam. The teacher was taken aback and asked, "Baruch, how did you manage to top the class in the exam?" I explained that I had been in Israel as a child and jokingly added that Hebrew was my mother tongue. She was pleasantly surprised.

Whereas the acceptance of Ethiopian Jews had made a modest inroad into the general public, this path stopped short at the army barracks gate. Most of the men didn't know my history. They thought I was an African, sent by my government to learn about military training. They started to call me "General Idi Amin Dada." Every month we took turns early in the morning to prepare the troop for the officer's inspection. When it was my turn, I told the men that when I commanded, "Stand!" they should respond, "Yes, sir, General Idi Amin Dada!" The officer arrived and that is what happened. I explained to him that this is what the men called me. People who came from all over the world were never taunted; I was the only one they picked on. I told him that I couldn't take it any more and that I needed a vacation. I know I manipulated him for my benefit. He did give me some time off, which I put to use working at the delicatessen.

I went back to continue my training and excelled at running, climbing, and jumping. The men said that I came by it honestly because I had just come out of the jungle. I learned to laugh it off and to "roll with the punches." Sometimes, however, insensitive officers created a hostile atmosphere by treating me as "different," not as equal as the others. One day one of them humiliated me so much, I ended up having a fist fight with him. I was thrown into the brig for twenty-four hours and then had to appear before a judge. I confessed to him that I didn't know what to do. "On the one hand, I am here in the army, dedicating my life for my country while my family is far away, and on the other hand, I am treated like I don't belong. What am I supposed to do?" The judge told me to go back to my unit and to stop getting into trouble. He threatened that if I did the same thing again I'd be put in jail for seventy-five days. He added, "Be careful."

Lecturers often came to our base from Hebrew University to acquaint us with a bit of the history of our country. One afternoon, a professor spoke about the immigrants who settled in Israel and how they established separate *yishuvim* (settlements), e.g., the Yemenites, the Moroccans, the Russians, and so on. A friend of mine asked him, "What about the Ethiopians?" He replied, "They claim they are Jewish, descendants of King Solomon, but they are not Jewish.. They have a religion like ours, but they don't look like us." I got so angry, I went up to the stage and said, "Are you a rabbi, that you know who is a Jew and who isn't? Where is it written in the Bible what color a Jew is? If it's true that I'm not Jewish, then I hereby resign from the army. Take my gun and release me right away." He got flustered and said, "I'm sorry, I'm sorry." A Russian immigrant yelled out, "Baruch, don't get mad. Sometimes it's better not to be a Jew." Everybody laughed and the tension was broken.

I did not have an easy time of it in the army. Nearly every day something happened to upset me. Some incidents triggered fights, like when a nasty guy insulted me, shoved me down, and pushed ahead of me in the dinner lineup. He had done this before, but this time I had had enough. I knocked him down. The men were amazed that I had the guts to tackle this loudmouth. The officer in charge, after having investigated the confrontation, let me go.

Most of the officers looked upon me as a troublemaker; yet when they asked for volunteers for dangerous missions, I was the first to raise my hand. Nobody really understood my devotion to Judaism and to Israel. They couldn't see it because of my color.

It was difficult to educate the people to accept us as real Jews. I found it hard to understand their distrust. I argued, "During our whole history, have the blacks ever harmed the Jews? Were I to come down from the mountain carrying the Ten Commandments like Moses, nobody would believe me. If I lived here for a hundred years, I'd still be called an Ethiopian, not an Israeli. While you may question your attitude to Judaism and Israel, I don't. I'm born with it; it's me, it's who I am."

Chapter VII

O ne day in 1977, when I was stationed near Jerusalem, I went into town to see what was happening there. At the central bus station, a man approached me and asked, "Are you from Ethiopia? Are you Baruch?" Then I recognized him. He was William (Bill) Halpern, whom I had met a long time ago in Yona Bogale's house in Addis Ababa. We embraced. He said he was happy to meet me then, because Dr. Graenum Berger, a fellow American who had devoted the latter part of his life to Ethiopian Jewry, was in Jerusalem to address the Knesset (parliament) on their behalf. Bill thought it would be mutually beneficial if I were to meet him. I agreed to go to his home, where I was introduced to the eminent social worker Dr. Graenum Berger, who was to become a lifelong friend.

Dr. Berger explained that when he had visited Ethiopia recently, the *kessim* had given him a letter asking for help; the condition of the Ethiopian Jews was going from bad to worse. And so he decided to address the members of the Knesset to solicit their intercession and assistance. He couldn't understand the resistance he met there. He asked me, "Do you know why the Israeli government is reluctant to accept your people?" "Yes," I answered, "it's because we are black; they think we are inferior and have nothing to contribute to the country. Also, they don't believe we are *real* Jews."

He wanted me to meet Professor Howard Lenhoff, president of his organization, the American Association of Ethiopian Jews (AAEJ), who was coming to Israel. He was a prominent marine biologist, based in California, and a personal friend of Ephraim Katzir, then president of Israel, who was also a well-known scientist. Lenhoff wired me to say when he would be arriving and advised me when he could see me. I gladly met with him. Later he invited me to join him for Shabbat at his family's home in Netanya. I stayed there for the weekend and we had long talks. He was very interested in what I had to say. He asked if I'd be willing to go to Bar-Ilan University to address a group of people, whom he would convene, to tell them my story and how I had come to Israel. I readily agreed.

I was asked a lot of questions at that meeting. It was a very emotional experience for me. I found myself dredging up from my memory a number of sad events. The people wanted to know how I felt about Israel; I told them the truth about how I had been treated and the problems I had encountered. But I assured them that this was my home, that – in spite of everything – I was proud to be there and that I wanted my family and the rest of Bet Yisrael to come there, too. A *Time* magazine reporter, "Bob," was in attendance and he took copious notes.

At that time, Prime Minister Begin had made a secret arrangement with the Ethiopian government to exchange army equipment for one hundred twenty-seven Ethiopian Jews to come to Israel. When the first new immigrants arrived in Jerusalem, they wanted to go directly to the Western Wall to pray. Bob asked me to go along with him to help take pictures of that momentous event; he was in the process of making a documentary in Israel. I accompanied him and we succeeded in taking some memorable photos. Unfortunately, Begin's project came to a sudden end when it became public in Geneva, where Moshe Dayan spoke openly about the "secret arrangement."

A few days later, Professor Lenhoff took me to meet the president of Israel and we three had lunch together. Although President

Katzir had no political power, he was keen to learn about my story and the predicament of the Ethiopian Jews. He concluded that "if the Falashas observe as Jews, believe they are Jews, and suffer as Jews, then to my mind, they are legitimate Jews" (loosely translated from the Hebrew).

Then Howard (Professor Lenhoff) brought me to his room at the Hebrew University, where he quizzed me about my escape from Ethiopia. He wanted to know if I could devise a way to rescue my people. "Yes," I replied, "we can definitely work something out to get them out as refugees via Sudan." We spent the whole night drafting a plan, which he gave to Prime Minister Begin, who passed it on to his military adviser, General Poran, who in turn submitted it to the Mossad. This was in March 1978. A couple of months later I got a call from Haim Halachmi of the Hebrew Immigrant Aid Society (HIAS) to meet with him and two Mossad agents at his office on Rehov Kaplan. After some discussion, they all agreed that my plan made sense. They asked me what I was doing at the time. I told them that I was in the army. The agents decided to wait until I finished my tour of duty.

Baruch in the IDF, 1977

Chapter VIII

Soon after I finished my stint in the army, I got a telegram from the Mossad to meet with them once again to continue our conversation regarding the Ethiopian Jews. I went to the same office as before; the three agents I had met previously were waiting for me plus another man, "Danny," who was to be in charge of the operation. After having examined other options, they decided to go ahead with the plans I had outlined. We discussed the many details this project would entail.

The men wanted me to go with them to Sudan to check out the situation. But there was a problem: I didn't have a valid passport. The Israelis had cut my Ethiopian passport in two when I had made *aliyah*. Since there was no Ethiopian embassy in Israel, we agreed that the best thing for me to do was to fly to Athens and once there I'd go to the embassy and claim that I had lost my document. I agreed to do this and sold my share of the deli. I put myself completely in the hands of the Mossad.

The Mossad men gave me strict instructions to go to a certain hotel in Athens. From there I was to call another Israeli, using his code name. When I got to that hotel, it was swarming with people in Arab dress. I figured that this must be the wrong place. I asked the driver if there was another hotel in the vicinity. "Yes," he said, and took me to a nearby location.

At the hotel reception I had to fill out a paper with my name, address, and other personal information, and also my passport number. I had the number of my mutilated and expired passport and filled it in. The idea was that I might later use this form to show that I had had a passport and claim that I lost it. This tactic should facilitate getting a renewal. The receptionist, a white man, started to speak to me in Arabic. He wanted to know if I was from Sudan – he had been born there – and he went on and on. Not wanting to attract attention, I begged his forgiveness, feigned illness, and told him I had to go to my room right away to lie down.

I called my contact and told him I was in another hotel. He started to scold me, "You have to follow instructions…" We arranged to meet the next day in the first hotel. I looked out onto the parking lot and noticed a man walking discreetly towards the entrance. I knew instinctively that this was my man. I walked over to him and said, "*Shalom.*" He was surprised and asked, "How do you know me?" I introduced myself. He scrutinized the lobby and after seeing the hubbub there, agreed to come over to my hotel. He was most impressed with the tranquility of the place and told me to stay there. His main instruction to me was to leave no stone unturned until I got an Ethiopian passport.

I went to a kind of club-café in Athens where I knew that Ethiopians hung out. I thought I'd ask around for ideas of how to speed up the passport process. I met an old friend, who advised me against saying that I had lost my passport. He said, "If you do it that way it would take a year until they check out the number, your history, etc. If I were you, I'd go to the embassy, show them what Israel had done to my passport, and ask for a new one."

I checked this plan out with my contact and he told me to go ahead with it. I went to the Ethiopian embassy, did as my friend suggested, and told them that I was a seaman and needed to have a passport as soon as possible. The clerk agreed that I should have the new red passport put out by the Communist regime. He told me to bring a letter from the shipping company and he'd see what he could do. A friend brought me to a shipping company and, for a nominal fee, the clerk wrote a letter stating that I was employed by them, that the ship was leaving in a few days and, if at all possible, to give me a passport before then. I asked the man to write the letter in Greek to confuse matters a little, even though it was translated by an interpreter in the embassy office. I got the passport in three days.

I reported back to my contact. He was surprised that I had gotten the document so soon. The Israelis had allotted me a whole month to do the job. When I reread my passport very carefully, however, I noticed a serious error. For "Place of Residence" they had written "Israel." I ran back to the office and told them that this would not do. I would never be admitted into Arab countries with that address. I asked the man to change it. He said, "No problem, I'll white it out and put Gondar Province, as you requested." I said, "No, if immigration officers noticed that something was erased, I'd be in serious trouble. Please make me a new one." He said, "Why do you want to spend money on a new one? Better give the money to the starving people in Ethiopia." I replied, "Don't worry, I'll pay for a new one and I promise to bring you my next salary to send back home." (Unfortunately, I never went back to the embassy.) He made out my new passport on the spot.

Now I needed a visa to enter Sudan. I knew of a club-café where Sudanese men gathered – just as Ethiopians got together in the other one. I went in, ordered a cup of tea, and looked around for someone to talk to. I introduced myself to a kind-looking man and told him I was from Eritrea. I said that I had a brother who was a refugee in Sudan and I needed a visa to go there to get him out. I asked him if he knew of a quick way I could get one. He pointed out a man who was a secretary in the consulate of Sudan and suggested he might be able to help me.

I waited until I saw this man leaving, and nonchalantly ambled over to him and started to walk out with him, all the while making small talk; I told him, in Arabic, that I was Eritrean and asked about the Eritrean community in Athens, where they were located, how large it was, etc. After we warmed up to each other, I mentioned that I had a brother who was suffering in a refugee camp in Sudan, but I didn't know how to get a visa to go and visit him. He said, "Why don't you come to my office and we'll discuss it?" He gave me his card and we each went our separate ways.

I returned to my hotel and reported to my Mossad connection what had happened. He said approvingly, "Good. Go ahead."

When I got to the man's office, he welcomed me with open arms. He told me, however, that he couldn't give me a visa there, for this was only a consulate, not an embassy. He would have to send the application for a visa directly to Sudan. When I inquired how long this might take, he sighed and said, "A long time." I told him I was on leave for just a month from a shipping company and asked if there was any way to speed things up. He thought for a while and said, "I know someone who is flying to Sudan tomorrow. Fill out the form and I'll have him deliver it to the proper department as soon as he gets there. They will in turn send the visa to me and you should have it within two weeks." I was very happy to go along with this plan. I thanked him profusely and filled out the form. I waited at my hotel and, sure enough, two weeks later I got a call from the consulate saying that my visa had arrived.

I picked up the document and now I was all set. I had my Ethiopian passport and my Sudanese visa; everything was in order. The plan was to go to Paris, meet my party there, and we'd go together to Sudan to fulfill our mission. But when I reported to the Athens Mossad agent that I was ready to fly to Paris, he announced, "Plans have changed. It's one o'clock now – you have to catch the five o'clock flight to Israel. They want to talk to you. They need more details." I was downhearted; I wanted so much to get on with my task. But this time I had to follow orders. I hurriedly packed my belongings, ready to leave. He picked me up, drove to the El Al office where he bought me a ticket, then delivered me to the airport and wished me a safe journey.

Chapter ıx

At the airport a beautiful lady sitting a few rows away smiled at me and then came over to sit beside me. I immediately became suspicious; somehow I didn't trust her. She introduced herself and told me she was of Greek origin but was living in Canada. Her name was Roulah and she was on her way to Israel to visit a dear friend who, she said, would become my future wife. I winced. She wanted to know my story. I told her I came from Africa, from the bush and the jungle. She laughed. But I became even more leery and, when the chance presented itself, I asked the security guard to check her out.

A female officer came over, took her to a ladies' room and checked her thoroughly and couldn't find anything amiss. When Roulah came back, she was very upset; she couldn't understand why they had picked on her. I told her that they did the same to me; Israel has many enemies and they must take every precaution to ensure everyone's safety.

While I was looking for my assigned seat on the plane, she stopped me as I was passing and asked me to sit near her. I told her I was heading for the smoking section. She said, "I smoke, too. I'll join you." We talked some more and she told me she was a well-known psychic. She repeated her intuitive remark that I was going to marry Susan, the Canadian Jewish girl with whom she was going to stay in Haifa. I laughed it off.

When we disembarked in Tel Aviv, Roulah tried to call Susan, but there was no response. She didn't know what to do. I suggested that she come with me in my taxi to Herzliya, which is halfway there, and then she could proceed on by herself to Haifa. She agreed, but when we got to my place, she tried Susan again and still got no answer. What to do? I gave her two choices: she could either stay at a nearby hotel or at my home; I had an extra room because my housemate was away. She opted for staying at my place.

Roulah was impressed with my location so close to the beach. When she saw the rising moon reflected in the sea in all its splendor, she stood there entranced – this was a spectacle she would never see in Canada. She was so taken with the setup that she asked if she might bring her friend to come and stay with us for a while, too. I had no objection. Roulah left her bags at my house and went off in a taxi and returned later – in the same taxi – with her good friend, Susan (Suzie) Migicovsky.

When Susan entered the room, I felt like I had been struck by lightning; an electric shock jolted my whole being. It was love at first sight. Not only was she beautiful, but she was Jewish as well – a very important criterion for me. The girls stayed with me for two weeks, during which time we did a lot of talking.

Roulah was determined to go to Hollywood to try her luck at acting and made an effort to persuade Susan to go along with her. Susan, however, declined; tired of the French nationalist politics in the province of Quebec, she had opted for *aliyah*. She had decided to make Israel her new home. Suzie was very much aware that she was part of the famous General Moshe Dayan's family and was keen to learn more about her heritage and the land of Israel. In order to do this, she attended Hebrew classes at an *ulpan* near her place in Haifa.

After having taken a disappointed Roulah to the airport, Susan wanted to go right back to Haifa to continue her studies at the *ulpan*. I pleaded with her not to go back just then on the grounds that it was too dangerous to travel so late at night, and I persuaded her to come back to my house. We were very attracted to each other and now that we were alone, we became romantically involved. Every day Susan would take a taxi to her classes in Haifa and come back in the evening so that we'd be together. I convinced her to switch to an *ulpan* closer to home, which she did.

This arrangement worked out very well until my housemate came home. At that point Susan and I decided to find a place of our own. We rented an apartment in Ramat Gan, where Susan was able to continue her studies at another *ulpan* in Tel Aviv. We were very happy.

Chapter x

I
n December I received a lovely Christmas card from Roulah, at the old address, in which she invited me and Susan to come to spend the holidays with her in Montreal. We wrote back to thank her and told her that we were living together in a new place. Apparently she was shocked. I can't imagine why, because it was she who had predicted the whole affair. Susan suspected that Roulah was in love with me. In any case, Roulah took Susan's letter to her family and told them she was living with a black man.

All hell broke loose! Suzie's family got hold of her and ranted and raved. They called her the black sheep of the family and ordered her to break off the relationship immediately. Suzie was so upset, she cried and cried. I couldn't bear to see her so miserable. I offered to call her parents and speak to them.

We went to a public phone and amidst the taunting of impatient people waiting in line, I spoke to her mother and said, "Why do you make your daughter cry? If you want her to go back, I'll send her home at my expense. I don't want Suzie to break her ties with her family because of me." Her mother hemmed and hawed. I told Suzie that I didn't want to come between her and her family and she should decide what she wanted to do.

Suzie wrote a long letter to her parents explaining who I was. She told them about my history and my devotion to Israel. The family took the letter to a rabbi in Montreal, who affirmed that there were black Jews in Israel and – if my story was true – that I was Jewish. They still were not appeased.

We decided to get married. I was thrilled! We went to a rabbi to get our certificate, but there was a problem – not for Suzie, but for me. The rabbi acknowledged that she was Jewish, without any documentation whatsoever. As for me, although I had papers stating that I was a Jewish Israeli, the rabbi didn't acknowledge them. This was despite the fact that both leading Israeli rabbis, Sephardi Chief Rabbi Ovadia Yosef (in 1973) and Ashkenazi Chief Rabbi Shlomo Goren (in 1975), had accepted that we, the Bet Israel, were bona fide Jews, and despite the fact that furthermore I had undergone a symbolic conversion in my youth.

The rabbi began asking me questions, like, "What is your profession?" I answered, "I'm a street cleaner, what's the problem?" He said, "Tegegne is not a Jewish name." I retorted, "Is Migicovsky a Jewish name? Can you show it to me in the Bible?" He said, "Get a letter from your parents stating that they are Jewish and then I'll marry you." I told him, "I don't know where my parents are; I've lost contact with them. But let me ask you a question: when you marry survivors of the Holocaust, do you ask them to bring you letters from the grave stating they are Jewish? If they don't have to, neither should I. Not every Jew who comes to Israel has parents to prove it."

He still refused to marry us. My temper started to rise. I said, "One of the first commandments that God gave us was *pru u'rvu* (go forth and multiply); you are pro-genocide." I became even angrier, grasped him by the beard, and shouted, "*You* are not kosher enough for *me*!" I took Suzie by the hand and we stormed out. So Suzie and I continued to live together "in sin" thanks to the rabbinate.

Chapter XI

Bureaucracy was blocking me in other arenas as well. When I came back to Israel from Athens in 1979, I went to the Mossad to find out what was going on. They informed me that the project was canceled. I was dumbfounded. "Why?" I asked. The agent answered, "It was a government order to drop the whole project." No further explanation. I had laid out a lot of my own money, so I gave them my expense account. They asked for my Ethiopian passport, which they confiscated, but they didn't pay me my money. They sent me to Haim Halachmi at HIAS to collect what I was owed, but there they gave me the runaround for three months.

Finally I lost my patience. I went into the HIAS office, overturned the official's table, and demanded my payment. He shouted at me, "GET OUT or I'll call the police." I said, "Fine, call the police – and while you're at it, get a policeman for me, too. It's bad enough that my people are starving in Africa, you want me to starve, too? I'm not leaving until I get my money." He said that Yehuda Dominitz, director general of the Aliyah Department of the Jewish Agency, was out of the country and he had no budget allocation for me. He advised me to meet with Danny, who was at a nearby café. I rushed out to meet him and when I told Danny my problem – that it had been three months since I was promised the

148

money – he brought me to his office and immediately sat down at his desk and wrote me a check. And that was the end of that.

I didn't let the matter of the failed rescue rest. I found out later that the agent, my contact, had gone to see my friend in Sudan, Ferede Azezewu Aklum, whose address I had given him. Apparently Ferede introduced him to five Jews in the refugee camp. The agent concluded that Israel didn't have to get involved in this matter. He said that he would look after them himself, through the UN. Later, when I was in Israel and heard what had happened – that he had found only five people wanting to leave and that there were no more Jews there – I cried out, "It's not true! This man (Ferede) must have been afraid to tell you the truth."

"I'm very sorry, Baruch," the Mossad agent said. "I would like to save as many Jews as possible, whether they're black, blue, or white…" I interrupted, saying, "If you were in my shoes and knew your parents were in danger and you had a way to save them, what would you do? You blame the whole world for not having come to the rescue of European Jews during World War II, and now you, who are my brothers, you tell me to let these people die? " He apologized again and said meekly, "Those were my orders." I felt so dejected, I started to cry.

I was at loose ends. I didn't know where to turn. A few days later I received a call from Professor Lenhoff asking me what was happening with the project. I informed him that it was canceled. He was very disappointed. He couldn't understand why they had abandoned the plan when I was prepared to take the risk of going there to try to open a door through which we could save Ethiopian Jews. He asked me, "If I got the financial backing, could you do it on your own?" I replied, "It's too dangerous for me to go alone. Many people know me in Sudan and, if you recall, I was almost imprisoned there. If anything happened to me, everything would collapse." He asked, "Who do you suggest could help you?" I answered, "Bill Halpern."

Lenhoff sent Bill to Israel and we laid out a plan. I began to feel a little more hopeful. I went to the Mossad and asked them for my Ethiopian passport, which they had taken from me. The agent wanted to know why I needed it, so I told him honestly what I intended to do. He didn't say anything, but picked up the phone and called his superior to come in. After I had explained to the boss what my plans were, he began to yell at me: "You are a citizen of Israel. You served in the army. You can't go to Sudan without permission. You know that." I said, "Yes, but it's for *pikuach nefesh*. It's a matter of saving my family." The decibel level rose when he said, "If you try to leave the country via the airport, I'm warning you: I'll have you arrested so fast you won't know what hit you. Then I'll put you in jail in that cell with the Japanese terrorist we arrested, who is now in a prison in Ramallah." Needless to say, they didn't give me back my passport.

I wasn't fazed by his tantrum. I thought, however, that the only way he could really stop me was if I left the country without an army permit, a required document for ex-service men. So I asked him, "OK, what do you want?" His response was very stern. He said, "If you have any more contact with the Americans, you must let us know immediately. If you receive a letter or any other communication, bring it to us right away. And furthermore, you are not allowed to have any more demonstrations." He thought I was like the other Ethiopians, obedient and submissive. He didn't know I had crossed the Sahara and was hardened against all obstacles. I bade him *Shalom*.

The next day I went to the army offices and asked them for an exit permit. When they asked why I needed it, I told them it was "to save my people." No problem; they gave me one on the spot – not for Sudan, but for Europe.

My next plan was to go to Athens to get another Ethiopian passport. I met with Bill again and instructed him to go to Jerusalem to get me a ticket for a flight to Rome, just in case the Mossad was waiting for me at the Athens airport. He delivered the ticket to me at a prearranged secret place. I explained to him that from now on we must sever all connections. He was to fly to Italy first and I would meet him there. I made an appointment with the Mossad agent to see me in his office at the exact same time I was to leave for Italy. When I got to the airport, I must admit I was terrified – I wasn't sure if I was being followed, or if the airport had been alerted, or who knew what I was up to.

Fortunately I got through with no trouble at all. I flew to Rome and met Bill at our appointed place. Bill, however, was fit to be tied; he had lost his bags with all his papers. He became slightly paranoid; he thought the Mossad had something to do with it, but as it happened it was a normal sort of mismanagement. We spent the night together in a hotel and made our plans. He agreed to go to Sudan first, to meet with my Ethiopian friend, Ferede, and to start investigating how best to proceed.

Ferede Azezewu Aklum had been a teacher in a Jewish school in Ethiopia. When Graenum Berger was there, he met Ferede and gave him his US address. Later, when Ferede became a refugee in Sudan, he wrote to Dr. Berger, who then forwarded Ferede's address to us. The Mossad agent had gone to see Ferede in Sudan, but Ferede, having learned to be suspicious of everyone, had given him no pertinent information. The agent had promised to come back for him and his five friends, but never did. When Bill arrived in Sudan, he went to see Ferede and met with him and eight other Ethiopian Jews we had referred to him.

I had to get to Athens, but didn't want to chance going by air. I feared the Mossad would be on my trail. From Rome I went by train to Bari, in southern Italy, where I embarked on a boat to Greece. In Athens I went to an American Express office and notified Bill where I was and how to reach me there. This was the safest way we were able to communicate with each other, via an American Express post office number. Bill responded that he had met Ferede and had given him three thousand dollars for food and shelter for his people. But nobody trusted him, because he was an American and unknown to them. He pleaded with me to come there as soon as possible.

Now I had to go back to Sudan, but didn't have the required papers. I hurriedly went to the Ethiopian embassy in Athens and told them I had lost my passport and needed a new one. They wanted a police report to that effect. I went to the police station in Blaca and told them I had lost my seaman's passport – to make it more plausible. They wanted me to search at the last five places I had been to. I went to an all-night disco in the tourist area, a taxi company, a bus company, a grocery store, and a café, and had them each sign a statement (in Greek to confuse the issue) that they didn't find my papers. I brought back my report to the embassy and waited for my new passport.

With Dr. Graenum and Emma Berger, 1992 (Photo Courtesy Yvonne Margo)

Chapter XII

Meanwhile, Suzie flew over and joined me in Athens. We spent a wonderful two weeks together holidaying in the islands. When we returned to Athens, my document was waiting for me. I paid the required sum and got my new Ethiopian passport without any more hassles. Now all I needed was a Sudanese visa. Although they had a Sudanese consulate in Athens, I knew it would take too long for them to process my request, and furthermore, they would have to send the forms back to Sudan, and I feared they would investigate my past. I was still "wanted" there and I would be denied entry.

In spite of the risk to my life, I was determined to proceed with my rescue mission. I decided to go to the Sudanese embassy in Rome, where they had the power to grant visas on the spot. So Suzie and I went to Rome by boat, reversing the way I had come to Greece, and there, with the help of a friend who worked in their office, the Sudanese embassy granted me a visa in three days.

I telephoned Bill at the Meridian Hotel in Sudan to tell him that I was all ready to go there. He mentioned that he was about to move from the hotel to live with an American friend who was working at the embassy. He assured me that he would leave his new address at the hotel's reception desk.

Before I left, Susan flew back to Israel, where I had authorized her to have sole control of our joint bank account. Then she returned to Rome to be where we could safely communicate with each other. I introduced her to one of my cousins, the then Ethiopian ambassador to Rome, who offered to take her into his home and to help her with anything she needed. Feeling that Susan was in good hands, I took off for Sudan.

In Khartoum, I stayed in a small, dinky hotel, at fifty cents a day, in order to save every penny. My room was close to the toilet; it was dirty and smelly, but I hadn't gone there to have a good time – I had a mission to accomplish.

I met up with Bill at a new address, where he told me all the difficulties he was having. He had gone to Gedaref and found eight people, five of whom had been waiting to be rescued by the Mossad man who never came through. Bill suspected that there were many more who wanted to leave, but realized that they wouldn't confide in him – they didn't really know him and didn't trust him – so he sent Ferede to Gedaref to speak to them. He brought them back with him to Khartoum. Through them and other contacts I had established who helped spread the word, we found another eighty-nine Bet Yisrael who wanted to make *aliyah*. Ferede and I met in my hotel room and stayed up all night discussing what to do. We decided to bring all the people to Khartoum, and made plans to feed and shelter them until they would be rescued.

I sent the list of the ninety-seven to Dr. Graenum Berger and Professor Howard Lenhoff. Dr. Berger had become interested in the Ethiopian Jews since his visit to Kfar Batya in 1955. In 1974, he initiated discussions to unite the Friends of the Beta Israel (Falasha) Community in Israel, which had been organized by Jed Abraham in 1969, and the reactivated Pro-Falasha Committee, to form the American Association for Ethiopian Jews (AAEJ). I worked closely with three active members of this association at that time – Mrs. Edith Everett, Dr. Theodore Norman, and Mr. Henry Rosenberg – and they really didn't want to perform the whole rescue operation by themselves. Their intention was to show Israel that, if we, as two persons, were able to take out a few people, then they – as a country – could achieve much more. The Americans had allotted us a budget of ten thousand dollars, which barely covered the costs of travel, hotels, and care for the refugees.

Dr. Berger and Professor Lenhoff sent our list of Jews in Sudan to the Jewish Agency in Israel, who took over the operation. (We knew there were really more Jewish people scattered throughout Ethiopia who wanted to go to Israel but weren't on the list, but this was at least a first step.) The Mossad sent their agent, Danny, to meet us in Bill's room with the list. He said he wanted to see the people, to interview them and make sure they were Jewish. He stated emphatically that he was not allowed to talk to me and said, "Just introduce me to the people and I will take care of everything." I retorted, "You don't know Sudan. I was here before you – Sudan is hell. As you see, I didn't come here for my pleasure. I am here to save my brothers and my sisters. Why do you say now that I'm not allowed to do it?" He replied, "Don't ask me, those are my orders."

I reluctantly conceded, "If you can do it, it's okay with me; that's all I want. I'm not important here – they are the important ones." But at that moment, I felt my heart drop. In spite of the fact that I had given in to him, I knew that I really was important. I suspected that this was Israel's doing. It seems that they really didn't want too many of us Ethiopians in their midst. This thought poured salt on my wounds.

After having investigated the refugees, Danny agreed to rescue only thirty-two of the ninety-seven on the list. He got passports from the UN and arranged to take them out of Sudan and then have them picked up and flown to Israel. Although I was upset at how I had been treated, I admired Danny very much for whatever he did accomplish and was grateful to him for all his efforts.

Despite my instructions, Bill and I had to figure out a safe way to get more people out of Ethiopia and into Sudan. I wasn't afraid to disobey the Mossad – fear never played a role in performing my duty. At times I had disagreements with Bill as to which parties to involve. He wanted to go about it in the American way, by asking

Christian or Muslim or humanitarian organizations to assist us, but I was sure that going that route wouldn't work. I knew that we needed two kinds of protection: one on the Ethiopian side to get people across the border and one in Sudan, after the refugees entered the country.

Bill and I kept ourselves separate from each other so as not to arouse suspicion. I was dressed like a Sudanese, in a *djellaba*. My strategy was to get an established organization to protect our people coming out of Ethiopia. There were the Communists, the Feudalists, the Eritrean Liberation Front (ELF), and others. I knew most of the members of these groups, but sensed that the Eritreans, who were powerful and well accepted in Sudan, would be most suitable. I made arrangements with them.

Also, on the other side, I needed the support of The Ethiopian Democratic Union (EDU), an association which controlled the area from Gondar Province to the Sudanese border. Fortunately, Shambel Belay of the EDU was in charge of the border. He was the nephew of Ras Wibenech (the Ethiopian Army veteran whose unit was saved by Falasha soldiers in WWII) and had connections with the Jewish people, as he had married a Jewish woman and had children living in Israel. His assistant, Mesafent Ferede, who was in control of the EDU army, was also very supportive. He paid dearly for this – he was later beaten and tortured for his involvement. We will always be grateful to him for his protection and assistance.

I wrote a letter to Shambel and delivered it personally. I asked for his help in getting my family across the border. Upon receiving my plea, he replied immediately that he would allow two hundred fifty people to cross over as soon as possible. I felt confident now that my kinfolk would be protected from all kinds of rabble and thieves who might otherwise attack them. Before long, I arranged for a group to leave the dangerous situation in Ethiopia – people whose houses had been burnt and who were therefore quite anxious to get out.

However, I was left high and dry. Bill went back to the US to try to raise more money. The Americans didn't have a budget for me to follow through and the Israelis wanted me out of the picture altogether. My people, who had left Ethiopia trusting me, followed my instructions and were to arrive in Sudan tired and hungry, and now I was going to leave them in the lurch, penniless and without a place to stay. I felt dreadfully guilty. My energy was being sapped in the name of the State of Israel and I was terribly hurt. I became very, very sick. I was destitute and everything was going wrong. I was physically and morally drained. It was hard for me to believe that I would be abandoned while trying to save my brothers and sisters. Thankfully, the Eritreans and border people looked after me. They took me to a doctor who gave me some medication.

Nevertheless, I saw proof that it was really possible to get my people out of Ethiopia. All it took was good organization and money to pay the powers that be enough to feed and shelter each person and a little extra for their troubles. If you paid per person, then the Sudanese would encourage more people to come and that way they would make more money. Certainly, America and Israel could have raised the funds if they really wanted to – it was not that expensive.

Sudan was cooperative and had no problem granting exit permits. From there the refugees could have been flown to a friendly European or African airport and then off to Israel. Many more Bet Yisrael could have been saved. The Americans, however, felt that Israel should have taken over at that point and the Israelis, on the other hand, wanted to work the rescue their own way, which in the long run turned out to be much more costly.

When the refugees finally made it to Sudan, I was no longer there, but I learned that their situation was disastrous. Nobody had made provisions for their arrival, but I know from previous experience that the disaster could have been avoided, had they planned in advance. For example, at one time, Canadian Physicians Overseas for Refugees (CPOR), together with Save the Children, had established clinics in Sudan to help the Jewish refugees. Drs. Mark and Norman Doidge of CPOR had done much to heal the sick and, in general, to improve the living conditions in the camps.

One time they had sent Henry Gold, a young student whose parents were Holocaust survivors and who was dedicated to helping his people, from freezing Montreal to sweltering Sudan to work there. He noticed that the Jewish refugees were undernourished and then discovered that they were given only half the rations, while the administrator sold the rest for his own profit. Henry notified the Jewish Agency, and the situation was rectified immediately.

But now, my people – whom I was trying so hard to save – were dying from starvation. The survivors were exhausted from digging so many graves; moreover, they could not bury the Bet Yisrael in a Muslim or Christian cemetery and there was very little land available, so sometimes they had to bury their loved ones in their own tents. To add insult to injury, some people blamed me for their horrible predicament.

Chapter XIII

I was quite ill and I could do no more in Sudan without help that was not forthcoming. Suzie was waiting for me in Italy, and I had to go back. But I needed a visa to reenter the country and it was almost impossible to get one – there was a glut of refugees waiting to go there. I was told that I had to go back to my embassy to approve my passport, because there were so many forged ones around. I was, however, eager to avoid the Ethiopian embassy. When my Eritrean friend heard about my situation, he said, "Don't worry, there's no problem." He was very well accepted at the Italian embassy and arranged to get me a visa very quickly. When I went to the plane – another obstacle – the crew didn't want me to let me on board, I was so sick. But my Eritrean friend, Temsgen Tesfazion, convinced them to take me.

In Rome, I had no money for a taxi, so I hired a private car to chauffeur me to the Ethiopian embassy. I thought my cousin would bail me out, but neither he nor his wife was there. I told the driver I couldn't pay him and he started to curse me. I pleaded with him to come back later and I'd pay him then, but he didn't believe me. He went off calling me every vicious name in his vocabulary.

I made my way to my cousin's home, but Suzie wasn't to be found. The watchman told me she had rented an apartment not too far away. When my cousin came home he gave me money for a taxi to Suzie's new address. She wasn't there. I had no keys and sat dejectedly on the stoop waiting for her return. I was so sick that when she finally arrived she didn't recognize me. I called her name. She couldn't believe I was her own Baruch.

Suzie practically carried me into the apartment and had me lie down for a while. Later she took me to the hospital. The doctors couldn't find anything specifically wrong with me. I couldn't get this question out of my mind: How did I get to the impossible situation where the State of Israel and I were pitted against each other? I knew a great deal about Christian enemies, but how in the world did I get Jewish enemies? After a few days of rest and a lot of tender loving care, I started to feel better.

Now here I was, stuck in Italy. Israel had threatened to arrest and imprison me if I ever went back, because I had gone to Sudan without their permission. The American Association for Ethiopian Jews offered to help me, if I decided to go back to Israel, by providing me with a top-notch lawyer to fight my case. I felt I could defend myself. I hadn't broken any laws in Israel – I had gone on this treacherous mission in Sudan to save my people, for *pikuach nefesh*. As a matter of fact, in October 1979, Barbara Weinberg, a wealthy Los Angeles supporter of Israel, confronted Yehuda Dominitz of the Jewish Agency on my behalf. He explained that they had spoken of imprisonment in order to interrogate me; but he gave her his word that I would be allowed free entry into the country. I found out later that another friend of mine, in the Mossad, also pressured the government to get me reinstated.

Meanwhile, while I was trying to figure out what to do, I needed to earn some money for Suzie and me to live on. I became a middleman for Italians who sought to buy African merchandise. This job worked out quite well. It provided us with our necessities. Yet I wasn't happy; my brothers' souls were crying out to me. I had to find some way to help them. Going back to Israel was not the solution. There I would be prevented from pursuing my heartfelt responsibilities.

I wondered if I could work directly with the AAEJ and try to rally support from that direction. I asked my friend Professor Lenhoff if he could arrange a lecture tour for me in North America to explain our serious situation. He thought it was a good idea and set up a North American speaking tour for me.

In 1979 I made my first public appearance at the General Assembly (GA), which is an annual gathering of the United Jewish Communities (UJC), an umbrella group for the Jewish Federations of North America and various independent Jewish communities. That year the GA met in Montreal. I addressed Jewish leaders from far and wide at the Queen Elizabeth Hotel. Yona Bogale and his son, Zacharia, came in from Israel to participate. I became very emotional when I told the assembly that I had been witness to the plight of my people in the refugee camps. They had been living in misery in Ethiopia, then risked their lives to escape to Sudan by way of treacherous routes, and now were living in squalor, praying and waiting for deliverance to Israel; but nobody had come to their rescue. For 2,500 years we had dreamed of going to Jerusalem but now we were left alone, deserted.

"Is it because we are black?" I challenged. "Israel must stop looking at our color. All Jewish hearts are the same color. The bones of my people who have died in the desert on their way to the Holy Land are bleached white – the same color as those of all mankind." We had lost track of ten thousand of my kinfolk – we didn't know if they were alive or dead. I was so overwrought, I began to scream: "There is no future for the Jews in Ethiopia. You mustn't play politics with human lives. You can't say anymore that you don't know about it. You must help your brothers. Don't let us die!"

I may have made a fool of myself, but I didn't care. At least I brought the situation to light. Yona, who had been in Ethiopia just two weeks earlier, spoke at the end of the conference and in his quiet, polite manner, described the harrowing conditions he had seen there. Between the two of us, we succeeded in making the public more aware. But even though everybody now knew about the dire needs of my people, the leadership still refused to take action.

During the assembly, however, we had some workshops with members of the North American Jewish Students' Network. They opened their ears and their hearts to us and soon became very involved in our cause.

While I was in Montreal, with Suzie still in Italy, I arranged to have lunch with Suzie's parents at the Queen Elizabeth Hotel. Graenum Berger graciously agreed to accompany me. Mr. and Mrs. Migicovsky seemed to be wonderful people, but were concerned about having a "mixed marriage" in the family. They asked Dr. Berger how he felt about a white girl marrying a black man. His response was that he was opposed to any kind of racial discrimination, particularly by Jews against other Jews. To him what was most important was that the two people should have many common interests. He assured them that I was a good man, that I would be a good husband and father and would support them to the best of my ability. He also suggested that they, as parents, could do things to help us become acceptable to their family and friends. The Migicovskys kissed us both when they left.

At Lincoln Center with prominent American Jewish leaders when Argentinean human rights activist Jacob Timmerman received the Ben-Gurion Award in 1979

Chapter XIV

The AAEJ people told me that if I wanted to stay in the USA they would accommodate me. A very good friend of theirs, Nathan Shapiro, was willing to hire me and help me settle in Chicago. I went to New York with Graenum Berger after the GA in Montreal, where I enjoyed his and his wife Emma's hospitality for several days. He called Nathan (Nate) Shapiro, who welcomed me and gave me a job, a house, and a guide to show me around. Mr. Shapiro owned two factories; one that made soaps and perfume and another that manufactured furs. I worked alternately in each of these plants. He hired a lawyer to get me a green card so I could work there legally. Nate was an unassuming gentleman, very wonderful to me, and had no organizational or political affiliations. He just wanted to be helpful.

After a while Suzie joined us and Nate said he would find her a job, too. He was very fond of her and offered to pay all expenses for our wedding. We set a date, hired a rabbi, and invited Mr. and Mrs. Migicovsky to come. They declined, however. They wanted us to be married in Montreal, because they said their whole family was there and I had nobody anyway. We decided to honor their wishes and get married in Montreal at a later date.

On December 26, 1979, I received a formal letter from the State of Israel confirming my free status in that country.

Chapter XV

Nate was interested to know what the problem was in getting Jews out of Ethiopia. I filled him in on all the hardships I had gone through and the difficulties I had encountered with the Jewish Agency in Israel. They had taken me off the job, refused help from the Americans, and promised to take out a certain number of people every month; but to date, six months later, nobody had been rescued. He couldn't understand why the government didn't fulfill its commitment.

Then Nate asked if I could do him a personal favor: "If I financed it, could you bring out five Jews from Ethiopia?" "Yes I can do it!" I exclaimed. I mentioned to him that Zacharia Bogale, who was in charge of the Ethiopian Jewish community in Israel, should be asked to work with me. He had access to a list of 28,000 from the Jewish Agency, which specified which Ethiopians were actually Jewish, as one had to be a certified Jew to be given automatic Israeli citizenship. Mr. Shapiro agreed to my proposal and gave me ten thousand dollars to execute the plan.

I met with Zacharia in Italy and we set about outlining our strategy. The first thing we did was send some money to the refugees in Sudan via an agent we knew, who distributed it as per my instructions – x amount of money per family. Then we had to figure out how to get passports for them.

It was common knowledge that it was possible to get forged Ethiopian passports in Italy, but you had to order a minimum of four hundred. We ordered the total amount and sent them to Sudan where they were to complete the process, with photo, number, etc. I had a connection there who looked after everything for me, for a fixed rate per person. Everything went smoothly. We resolved to send the selected people from Sudan to Germany, because one didn't need a visa to go there.

Group in transit, Frankfurt, Germany 1980

Chapter XVI

I flew to Germany and waited there for the scheduled arrivals. The first group was made up of two sisters, their husbands, and a child each – six people in all. I was elated! We sent their names off to the Jewish Agency and they wired back to say that they were *not* Jewish. This was terrible. I called Nate Shapiro and asked him what to do. He suggested that, if it didn't work out there, I should bring them back with me to America. The Israelis claimed that they were prostitutes and other kinds of lowlifes. When I began to argue with them – we knew they were Jewish and were on the original list – they advised me to go to the Israeli Consulate in Bonn if I wished to discuss the matter further.

I was so disheartened, I didn't want to talk to them; I sent Zacharia instead. In the meantime, Germany offered these Ethiopians refugee status. When Israel finally agreed to accept them, they refused to go, since Israel had insulted and humiliated them so insensitively. They chose to remain in Germany and are there to this day.

The second set of arrivals consisted of two people: one man, who was on the list – one hundred percent stamped, sealed, and approved Jewish – and the other, a handsome teenager about fifteen or sixteen years old whom he claimed was a relative, who was not on the list. The man was sent off to Israel immediately, while the youth was given the option of staying in Germany or waiting in the airport while we tried to iron out his identity crisis. The boy feared he was being denied *aliyah* because his mother had been forced, out of sheer necessity, to work as a prostitute and he was deemed unclean. He didn't want to stay in Germany. He wanted only one thing: to go to Jerusalem. He was detained at the airport for three days, during which time he refused to eat or drink. Zacharia and I took turns watching over him.

On the fourth day, unfortunately, he was sent back to Sudan. Later we were devastated to learn that this young man had hanged himself upon his return. Nathan Shapiro and the members of the AAEJ were horrified when they heard the tragic news. Police were sent to investigate, but apparently the community covered up the whole episode.

Next a group of fifteen children came to Germany. All were on the list, except for one, whose brother was on it, yet he was not. I fought tooth and nail to get this boy accepted. With some probing, we were able to establish that his father was already living in Israel, and so the Agency relented. We rejoiced when all fifteen youngsters were airlifted to the Promised Land.

By now I had demonstrated that I, practically alone, was able to get twenty-two refugees out of Ethiopia. But the establishment still didn't want to acknowledge their failure to act and the possibility of rescuing more of my beleaguered kinfolk. Furthermore, they spread rumors that I was taking people out of Africa to sell them as slaves. Though my feelings were hurt, I was able to disregard these vile accusations. My only regret was that I had started to give hope to so many people and then was inadvertently stopped in my tracks. All I was able to achieve was to save a few individuals on a person-to-person basis, thanks to the generosity of Nathan Shapiro.

The AAEJ was prepared to publicize in the *New York Times* the sordid account of what was going on, to embarrass the powers that be, but I felt we should try other methods first. Nate, who felt guilty about the death of the young boy, decided to take an active role in the American Association for Ethiopian Jews. He put more money into the effort and he, together with the other committed members, began to make things happen. Soon with help from my contacts, we were able to rescue another three hundred sixty Ethiopian Jews, who made their way out of the refugee camps via Kenya to Israel.

Demonstration in Washington, 1999

With US Senator Rudy Boschwitz, 1992

Chapter XVII

Suzie's parents insisted that we get married in Montreal. So we packed up and left Chicago to make a new life in Canada. Suzie and I were married on April 17, 1980, in a private ceremony officiated by Rabbi Kramer at the Adath Israel Synagogue. He said, "Although Kipling alleged that 'East is East, and West is West, and never the twain shall meet,' this is a great occasion where the East and West are actually meeting." I couldn't help thinking of my beloved grandfather's predictions that I'd travel all over the world and marry a white woman.

On July 28, 1981, Suzie gave birth to a beautiful baby girl, whom we called Yaffa. She was a delightful child and soon became the center of attention for the whole family. To this day I don't know if they came out of love for Yaffa or out of curiosity about her color. But come they did, at all times and at all hours. Many times, when I'd return home after a day's work and wanted to play with my little girl, I couldn't get near her – there were too many people around. Besides, the room was so full of toys, it was often hard to find her among all the other dolls. It was all so strange to me. We had never known of toys in Ethiopia.

Suzie and I set up a small business, running a snack bar in an industrial center. We lived upstairs, and even though Suzie and I worked night and day trying to make a go of it, it didn't do very well. To add to our income, I took a job as a superintendent in a private Jewish school.

Susan Migicovsky and Baruch Tegegne, married 1980

Chapter XVIII

W hile living in Montreal, I became involved with people I had met at the General Assembly, who became active on behalf of Ethiopian Jews. Young men like Mark Zarecki and Herb Weinstein of the North American Jewish Students' Network (NAJSN) and the esteemed Rabbi Hausman, who came as an interested individual, threw themselves into the thankless job of lobbying the Jewish community for their rescue. Simcha Jacobovici, a strong individual and chairperson of the network, was born in Israel and was familiar with the situation. He was very keen on helping his fellow Jews, because his father's whole family had perished in the Holocaust. His father was the lone survivor. Simcha and I became very good friends. He arranged for me to speak in numerous places, where I succeeded in reaching the hearts of many young men and women.

Once, when I spoke in Washington to the Students' Network at the General Assembly, a bright Canadian medical student, Mark Doidge, and his brother, Dr. Norman Doidge, approached me and asked, "What can we do to help?" Mark offered to be available whenever I needed him. During a school break, he came to Montreal and we sat down to discuss how best to proceed. He was eager, enthusiastic, and came up with some very good ideas.

We agreed that he'd begin by offering workshops at his home

on Spadina Avenue, in Toronto. We set down guidelines and decided to broaden our base. We invited Professor Irwin Cotler, member of the NAJSN, and Professor Edelman, who headed "Project Lifeline," which had brought sixty thousand Vietnamese refugees to Canada, to meet with us. I also asked young Professor Bruce Gottlieb, whose father had been to Ethiopia, to join us. Together we formed the Canadian Association for Ethiopian Jews.

With Martin Luther King III, Montreal, 1998

Chapter XIX

The Canadian Jewish Congress was opposed to our efforts to save Ethiopian Jews. They didn't want any other organization collecting money for a Jewish cause. They believed that Israel was on top of the situation and we shouldn't meddle in their affairs. We had thought that Dr. Edelman, who was experienced in saving refugees, would help us, but he decided to go along with Congress's policy. Irwin Cotler, who had been elected to the CJC by eight hundred students as their representative, was torn between his promise to support the Canadian Association for Ethiopian Jews and the CJC politics.

Though our association agreed with much of what Congress did, we were dismayed by the fact that, while we were bickering back and forth, my people were dying. Matters between us and Congress came to a head. We met in Kingston (halfway between Toronto and Montreal) and tried to iron out our differences, but to no avail. CAEJ then broke all ties with the CJC.

In 1982, when Israeli Prime Minister Begin came to Detroit to address the General Assembly, we organized a huge demonstration. Between the Students' Network and CAEJ, six hundred young people came out and threatened to go on a hunger strike. We tried to prevent Begin from speaking. We asked the committee to let the students address the assembly, but were turned down. What to do?

We stopped the demonstration temporarily and attended a workshop organized by the students. There we distributed pertinent information and I spoke to the participants. Soon they passed a resolution demanding that I be given authorization to speak to the General Assembly. But I wasn't on the agenda.

We thought of a ploy to get me onto the platform. We decided to buy Begin a present, and then, upon presenting it to him, I would ask the prime minister to say a prayer for the Jews of Ethiopia and perhaps grab the microphone and make my plea. They left it up to me to do whatever I thought was right.

We bought the present, but before I could give it to Begin, I was stopped by someone who came to take it from me. When the students saw this, they started to chant, "Let Baruch speak! Let Baruch speak!" This nearly turned into a riot. The police appeared and several students were taken into custody.

Later, I learned that Begin had told a mutual friend that when he was young he was worse than we were. He agreed that we had to do everything in our power for *pikuach nefesh*. He admired our persistence and instructed the GA to have the police release all the detainees. At the end of the session, Begin prayed for all the Jews and devoted an extra four minutes to the Jews of Ethiopia.

It was during this conference that for the first time the whole issue of the plight of my people was brought to world attention. Moreover, the US Congress and Senate each set up a committee to deal with the whole situation. I later attended some Senate hearings in Washington with a few senators, including Senator Boschwitz, who became active in our cause.

Chapter xx

I had been working with three groups: the American Association for Ethiopian Jews (AAEJ), the Canadian Association for Ethiopian Jews (CAEJ), and the North American Jewish Students' Network (NAJSN). I wasn't concerned with politics; I worked with any organization that would help my people. We had less and less to do with the Canadian Jewish Congress. As a matter of fact, its executive director, Alan Rose, had offered me a scholarship to go back to school and advised me to drop the whole issue.

Soon it became obvious that Congress was becoming even more antagonistic towards CAEJ. The Israeli ambassador went so far as to say that our information was not true. The CJC did help several Ethiopian Jews who came to Montreal, but that was the extent of their involvement.

We had reached a critical moment in our efforts. It looked like we were losing support. The community believed that Israel was taking care of everything and there was nothing more to do. Yet we knew that every day we were losing lives. Simcha Jacobovici, who was passionate on the subject, said, "Instead of fighting, let's change tactics." He came up with the brilliant idea of making a documentary film to expose the truth. But where would we get the money? He laid out a plan. We formed a company through which he solicited funds: from the United Nations to film refugee camps in Sudan; from the Ministry of Tourism in Ethiopia to show off the country's beautiful culture and landscape; and from the Canadian Broadcasting Corporation, who would own the documentary upon its completion.

The UN sent twelve thousand dollars, the Ethiopian Ministry offered to provide airfare for four people from England to Addis Ababa plus a tour guide, and the CBC gave us twelve thousand dollars. We were on our way! Although I was *persona non grata* in Ethiopia, I arranged the whole trip; I outlined an itinerary for the crew, gave them names of people to see, and suggested ways of approaching them.

I cautioned Simcha and the others not to say that they'd come to Ethiopia to film Jews. I recommended they say that they were there to film all the different communities: Muslims, Christians, etc. They were very successful in what they did. They were warned not to take pictures of the Jews, but managed to take some anyhow. Then they went to Sudan and filmed the people in the refugee camps.

In Israel the crew interviewed Prime Minister Yitzhak Rabin and different ministers to see what their reactions were to the Ethiopian Jews. Many were indifferent, others didn't want to get involved, and a very small minority did want to do something. Debates raged in the Knesset. Simcha tried to show via his films the contribution the Ethiopians were making to building up the country. Some officials became so angry with the documentary that they threatened to destroy it; they said he couldn't leave the country with it. Simcha said, "All right, I'll call the press and television people and if you want to burn the film, you can do it in front of them. I've been to totalitarian countries and they didn't confiscate my film. Here, in democratic Israel, you want to destroy it!" They finally gave in and allowed Simcha to take the documentary back to Canada.

In 1983 the CBC and other major networks aired the film, *Falasha: Exile of the Black Jews*. Among other prizes, in 1985 it was awarded a Certificate of Special Merit by the Academy of Motion

Picture Arts and Sciences (the Academy Awards). At this point, the picture changed. People from all major Jewish organizations now saw clearly what was happening in Ethiopia. They demanded answers from their leaders. The response was that they hadn't been aware.

Alan Rose, executive director of the CJC in Montreal, took a trip to Ethiopia to "investigate" the problem, but was hosted by the authorities and was given questionable information. He reported that he didn't see any Jews in the hills, nor did he find any in the hotels. Though he admitted that there were some problems, he didn't want to criticize Israel. He stated that all was being taken care of and that he believed in "quiet diplomacy."

Israel sent Ethiopians to tour America to reassure everyone that they had the matter under control – that they were looking after everything. While all this was going on, around fifty of my people were dying every day. I was asked to go on TV to corroborate the emissaries' stories, but I refused, because they were not true.

By 1984, somehow seven thousand Ethiopians had come to Israel, through various means – with help from Americans, through the humanitarian organization CARE, or via Israelis. Most of them got there from Sudan by boat or by El Al, following routes I had outlined. I knew for certain that many more could have been saved. We learned later that four thousand of my people died from starvation and neglect.

Presenting letter to Stephen Lewis, Canadian Ambassador to the UN, in New York, 1983

177

Chapter XXI

I n the midst of all these controversies, we tried to bring some of our people out of Ethiopia into Canada. We would have preferred for them to go to Israel, but the Israelis were not acting fast enough. In 1980, with the help of Suzie's father, Al Migicovsky, who guaranteed that they wouldn't be a burden on society, we brought over a man who was desperately ill and needed medication. We also rescued three sisters – Devorah, Galilah, and Bethel – cousins of mine whose mother, Malka Avraham, had like me been sent in her youth to Israel to study at Kfar Batya. Dr. Isaac Gottlieb, the father of Bruce (who had helped me form the Canadian Association for Ethiopian Jews), met the three girls in London, put them up in a hotel for the night, then sent them on their way to Montreal the next day.

There was no community support to accommodate them when they arrived, so they stayed at our house for a year. The Quebec law stipulated that all immigrants had to attend French schools. Only those parents who could prove that they had an English education were permitted to send their children to English schools. As Suzie was officially the girls' sponsor, she fought for the right to register them in an English Jewish Day School. One of the main reasons we did all this was, again, to show that it could be done. Two years later, the girls' mother, Malka Avraham, arrived as well.

Dr. Bruce Gottlieb, who was very supportive through all this, told me about the services offered by the Jewish Immigrant Aid Society (JIAS). They assisted immigrants once they had arrived in Montreal. This information proved to be very helpful.

After the sisters had arrived, Bruce introduced me to Stan Cytrynbaum, who, with his wife, decided to foster Devorah; Mark Zarecki, of Hillel, chose Galila; and Edit Kuper took Bethel under her wing. The girls turned out to be real treasures and flourished in their new environment.

At the time of this writing, Devorah has a Phd in pharmacy; Galila has a doctorate in mathematics; and Bethel graduated from Yale and then earned a law degree from Harvard.

Then I managed to bring my sister, Malefia – without her husband (he was not allowed to leave at the time, but came later) – to Canada with two of her four daughters. The other two had already emigrated to Israel, and then another girl was born in Montreal. My sister and all her daughters were reunited in Montreal for a while, but the two Israelis opted to go back to the Holy Land, where they had begun to build a new life.

Our next endeavor was to bring five people from Sudan to Montreal. We were assisted by CAEJ and the Province of Quebec. This began with a phone call from a Madame Gagne, of the Quebec Department of Immigration. She said she had been looking for me and was glad to have finally found me. She told me that she had traveled to Sudan, had visited the refugee camps, and was appalled by the terrible conditions there. She wanted to help! She had called JIAS, but was told that their mandate did not include bringing people into the country. "Why not?" she asked. "You should support them."

Mme. Gagne was up in arms. She threatened to make a public scandal: "You help Russian Jews, we help you bring them in; why don't you help the Ethiopians?" I was so happy to have received this call from a government official. Soon, together with Mme. Gagne and Rifka Augenfeld of JIAS, who threw herself wholeheartedly into the task, we were able to bring some fifty families to Montreal.

Chapter XXII

CAEJ was working with the US as well. I had been invited by Barbara Gefen to address the Boston Hillel students and, after the session, she suggested I meet with the renowned human rights advocate Elie Wiesel. Her feeling was that if he supported our cause, it would be beneficial to all concerned.

Barbara made an appointment for us with the famous writer, speaker, and activist, at his office at Boston University. When we got there, I surmised by his accent that he must speak Hebrew, so I conversed with him in that language, because it was easier for me. I told him that I had read a great deal about his work regarding the Holocaust and human rights, but was surprised that he hadn't said or done anything about the plight of the Ethiopian Jews. He listened attentively and said that, in all honesty, he didn't know about it. He added that when he was a boy in Europe, he used to study the Kabala. That mystical book predicted that the *Mashiach* (Messiah) would come from Ethiopia. He was intrigued by what I had told him and asked us to give him some time to study the situation.

Within two weeks, Elie Wiesel wrote an article in a newspaper stating that he supported the all-out effort to rescue Ethiopian Jews. He then took a trip to Israel to investigate the issue firsthand. When he returned, he convened a meeting at Brandeis University to look at the matter from all sides. He invited the Israeli ambassador, several US Jewish leaders, an official from the State Department (in charge of refugees), Lisa Freud from the AAEJ, and me. I wasn't informed that there was to be a debate; I thought I was merely asked to attend a conference.

I was greeted warmly when I got there and was put up in a lovely hotel; the Israeli ambassador's room was just across the hall. When I came to the university the next morning, I was stunned to learn that I was part of a debating team; I hadn't prepared for it. There were thousands of students in the auditorium. I was slightly intimidated, to say the least.

Elie Wiesel opened the session telling everyone that he had been to Israel to check out what was going on regarding the Ethiopian Jews and was not satisfied with the answers he got from the government. That was why he had convened this panel – to learn more about the situation. We were to give our opening remarks at that time and the debate was to follow the next day.

Kieger, the US State Department official, said that the US was allowed a maximum of three thousand refugees – from no specific groups – to enter the country. He added that they had helped Israel liberate and settle Russian Jews, but were never asked to assist them with the Ethiopian Jews. As a matter of fact, the US had good relations with Sudan and Egypt and could probably work out some of the problems through official channels.

The Israeli ambassador said that he had grown up in Argentina as an active member of the Zionist Youth Movement. He remembered learning that there were Ethiopian Jews in Israel. He was certain that Israel was doing everything possible to help them. He was aware that there were children and workers there and couldn't understand what the problem was. I realized right away that he had been prepped by the minister of immigration and was just reiterating their position. I knew that the children he referred to were the selected few who had come to Israel to study (as I had done) and the workers he mentioned were there on work permits, whose passports were withheld and returned to them only when they went back to Ethiopia. They were not recognized as having made *aliyah* and were not given Israeli citizenship.

When I got up to speak, I said that I was not a politician, but if they wanted to hear how the Jews in Ethiopia survived, about life in the refugee camps, and the problems of emigrating to Israel, I was willing to talk about it. There was no time to pursue these matters then. A few others spoke and the proceedings adjourned till the next day's debate.

The debate took the form of questions and answers. After the Israeli ambassador had replied to a few queries, I was asked about the conditions in Ethiopia and in the refugee camps. I spoke frankly about my people's efforts to maintain their Judaism, the lack of freedom, the persecution, and the struggle for survival. I described the horrible conditions in the refugee camps: the filth, the hunger, and the deaths. When I related the difficulty in getting Israel to help us, people were incredulous, shocked, and astonished.

Elie Wiesel asked me, "Which was the first book you ever read?" I answered, "*Mizmor l'David* (the Psalms); all our children learnt that book practically by heart." He then went on to ask me when I was born, where I was brought up, and a few other details of my life.

After I had gone through some of my history, I confronted the Israeli ambassador. I asked him to translate and read to the audience the official policy towards refugees and *aliyah* of the government in 1973, 1975, 1978, and 1979, which he did most eloquently. It was very evident that there was no mention of any attempt by the government to rescue Ethiopian Jews. I posed this question: "Mr. Ambassador, how can you say to the public that you are doing your best for human rights, when nothing has been done for my people?" He became visibly angry and retorted, "Things have changed now." "No," I countered, "the same people are still in charge." "This is garbage," he bellowed, and threw his papers down on the floor.

The audience supported me. Elie Wiesel asked me where I got this natural talent. He said I could have been a lawyer or a politician. He came over and gave me a kiss! This established my credibility with the people. Later, the B'nai Brith and Hillel Foundation at Brandeis University presented me with the "Shifra and Puah Award,"* so named in honor of the two Hebrew midwives who had the courage to save many Jewish lives by defying the Pharaoh's command to kill all the newborn Hebrew babies (Exodus 1:16).

I happened to share a taxi to the airport with the Israeli ambassador. By then he had calmed down and suggested that I go back to Israel to continue my fight within the country. He even offered me a good position. I knew he had staged the fit of anger because he didn't like the way I embarrassed the State of Israel in public.

Thanks to Graenum Berger's selfless dedication and persistence, pressure mounted in the USA for more action. Some senators formed a committee to delve into the matter. They invited the Israeli consuls from New York and Washington, some other politicians, and me to a meeting. They asked the consul, Benjamin Avileah, why the Israeli government was not doing more for the Ethiopian Jews. He answered, "What's the rush? We're preparing absorption centers. Don't you know there's a housing shortage? They've waited twenty-five hundred years – they can wait a little longer."

When Senator Boschwitz heard these lame excuses, he exploded! He said that by this kind of inaction we lost six million of our people. In Ethiopia and Sudan our brothers were dying every day. This was no time for excuses. He threatened that if they didn't take out four hundred people every month, he'd expose the whole issue in the *New York Times*.

I really don't think the Israelis were being mean-spirited. In the midst of all their own problems, they were truly not aware of the Ethiopian issue. Throughout history, when Jewish communities were in trouble, they often had places to run to – other established communities were there to help. We had no one. It became incumbent on us to further publicize our predicament.

---

* See appendix 2.

Chapter XXIII

The movement in the USA was becoming very strong, not only in support of Ethiopian Jews, but of the Russians, as well. We staged large demonstrations in front of the Israeli consulates in New York, Washington, Los Angeles, and Montreal. I remember Senators Dole and Javitz and New York Mayor Ed Koch came over to talk to me at one of the protests. A while later we learned that Senator Javitz had gone off to Sudan to investigate the situation. Now the pressure on Israel to speed up immigration became unstoppable.

Israel defended itself by saying that there were seven thousand new arrivals in their country from Ethiopia enjoying life there. If things were so bad, they claimed, why weren't they complaining? The CAEJ and the AAEJ conceded that they had no valid argument against this assertion. I, however, suspected that something was terribly wrong. I asked the organizations to each send a delegate to come with me to Israel to find out what was going on.

Lisa Freud (AAEJ), Simcha Jacobovici (CAEJ), and I went off to Israel in 1984 to try to solve the puzzle. When we got there, we discovered that the Ethiopian Jewish community was divided into seventeen organizations, with many of them antagonistic against the others. I pleaded with them: "How can you do this? We have one cause – to save our brothers and sisters. Nothing else is important enough to keep us separated. We must unite and work together!" After much persuasion, they finally agreed. We also met with representatives from forty-four absorption centers. I was overjoyed to see them; yet I was distressed that there were no plans being made to accommodate those who were left behind. We wanted to visit some of the centers, but were told that we couldn't without permission from the Jewish Agency. The new arrivals were kept isolated and incommunicado from the rest of society.

When the forty-four representatives met with us, they were afraid to speak openly in front of Lisa and Simcha; they didn't trust white people. It took me a long time to convince them that my friends were on their side. That done, I had to use all my energy to persuade them to stand up and fight to save our people. It was a matter of life and death. They were frightened to do anything to jeopardize their status quo – in particular, the benefits they received from the government. I patiently explained that they were now living in a democracy and that they had every right to demonstrate and express their views. They excused themselves by saying that they didn't know how to go about it. We assured them that we would teach them.

The group of forty-four elected a committee to work with us. We opened an office in Ramat Gan, called Bet Yisrael, with the support of CAEJ, which covered the costs of the rent and the telephone. Our first task was to organize a demonstration. I worked day and night to map out all the details. We needed to hire buses, but had no budget. Thankfully, Lisa prevailed upon Nathan Shapiro to foot the bill. We got two thousand people to come out to demonstrate. At the bus terminal, we all gathered at the square and then, while marching to the prime minister's office, we passed the Binyanei Hauma Convention Center and noticed that the Zionist General Council was holding a huge conference. We felt that we must take advantage of this opportunity to alert their members of our cause. As time was running out, we made a quick decision to send half the demonstrators onward to the prime minister's office and the rest of us stayed right there and carried on our protest in front of Binyanei Hauma.

When I tried to go in to address the assembly, Chaim Aharoni, who was the assistant to Dominitz, head of the Jewish Agency, stopped me and said that I wasn't allowed to speak because I was Canadian. I pointed out to him that the hall was filled with Americans and Canadians. "No," he said, "we don't want you!" I countered, "We have survived for two thousand, five-hundred years in worse conditions. You're not going to stop our mission now; we'll be here whether you like it or not." A photographer later published a picture of us bickering. I looked so devilishly angry! The caption read: "He won't let me speak!"

I had no desire to make this a personal confrontation. Our purpose there was to save Ethiopian Jews, not to have a battle of egos. I asked Aharoni if he would accept an Israeli citizen of Ethiopian descent to address the people. To save face, he agreed to allow Joseph Wobah to speak. I made one specific request to him: that he release some of the people who had been arrested when they had tried to break out of their Israeli absorption center, where they had felt totally estranged. Some men, like Adisu Massala, were simply looking to get away from what seemed to them their incarceration. (Adisu Massala later became a member of the Israeli Knesset.) Aharoni called the chief of police immediately and they were all released. After a short briefing with our representative, we left abruptly in order to get to Prime Minister Shamir's office before it closed.

When all two thousand of us arrived at the PM's office, our suppressed feelings broke loose. A near riot ensued. People were jumping and falling and shouting and yelling. Ambulances shrieked and police sirens wailed. I couldn't believe the bedlam. An officer came over to me and asked who the leader was. I pointed to somebody else embroiled in the melee.

We met with Shamir and he promised he would do the best he could. He asked for a period of one month to concentrate on the issue. I thanked him, but reminded him that if nothing were done, we would continue our demonstrations.

I stayed in Israel for a month, becoming more and more involved in our cause. Suzie called and asked me when I was coming home. I told her that the people wanted me to stay one more month.

With Prime Minister Shamir and other Bet
Israel representatives, December 1981

In front of the prime minister's
office, Jerusalem, 1984

Chapter XXIV

A nd now I come to the saddest day of my life. Two weeks after I had spoken to Suzie, I received a lawyer's letter notifying me of our separation. I was so upset, I fell down on my desk. I phoned to talk to her, but couldn't make any headway. I immediately arranged to go home to persuade her to change her mind.

We had a painful meeting. Suzie had good reason to be angry. She told me that ever since we were married I was never home. She understood my dedication to my people, but stressed that she needed a husband and our daughter needed a father. I was devastated. I told her I would quit what I was doing and stay home and do anything she wanted. But Suzie looked at me and said, "No, Baruch. This is your life, your commitment. You *have* to do what you are doing. I don't want to stop you from saving lives. But I can't live like this; we will have to go our separate ways."

The divorce was very hard for Yaffa and, as difficult as it was, I decided to move to Toronto, just to be far away. I knew she needed her mother more than she needed me.

Our divorce was finalized in 1985.

Chapter xxv

soon returned to Israel. I had to finish my job. When I got there I
saw that there was a new crisis. There were conflicts between Bet
Yisrael's understanding of Jewish law and that of the rabbis.

For example, Israel does not have civil marriages – only religious unions are recognized by the State. As for my people, marriages performed by the *kessim* in Ethiopia were accepted by Israel
as legitimate. But immigrant Ethiopian couples who wanted to
wed in Israel were not allowed to, unless they first submitted to a
symbolic conversion. This embarrassed and confused the Ethiopians. They asked, "How can they do that to us? If our religious
marriages in Ethiopia are considered kosher, then why can't we
have a religious marriage here? How can we convert from Jewish
to Jewish?" There were no logical answers. Some Ethiopians took
this issue very much to heart; they felt there was something wrong
with them to make them so unacceptable. I know of one man who
became so despondent, he committed suicide.

Another bone of contention was the laws of *niddah*, which
deal with the ritual impurity of women during their menstruation
and after childbirth. According to Rabbinic tradition, husband and
wife are required to sleep apart – usually in separate beds – during
this period. In Ethiopia, however, women slept totally away from
the house. When the interval was over, the woman went to the

mikvah for a spiritually cleansing ritual bath. Modern secular Israelis don't observe these laws at all, and many of them don't even know about them. There was an incident in one of the absorption centers where a recent immigrant wanted his wife out of the house and the director didn't want to accommodate them. The man got very angry and the director threatened to punish him for his insolence. I was summoned and after rushing over I tried to explain what was happening. But there was nowhere for her to go. I solved the problem by setting up a tent behind the building.

The rites of Passover posed another problem. In Israel the holiday begins with a Seder – a festive meal. In Ethiopia, however, Bet Yisrael slaughtered an animal in preparation for the holiday. This custom was prohibited in Israel. We protested, and some of the authorities accepted our practice, but not all. Nevertheless, my people continue to perform this ritual.

It was very difficult to bridge the gap between the Israeli and Ethiopian practices. Despite our difficulties, I thanked God once again that we were living in a democracy where we could fight for our rights and against injustices. I organized demonstrations to protest the marriage restrictions and tried to convince the Ministry of Religious Affairs to go easy on my people. I explained that they mustn't hurt their pride by pushing them; they could help change their ways through understanding and education, by going step by step.

In the meantime, I went looking for a rabbi who would agree to marry members of Bet Yisrael. I solicited many who were afraid to go against the tide, but I finally met Rabbi Shloosh, chief rabbi of Netanya, who did not hesitate for a moment. He had done research and had written a book in which he stated that, in his opinion, it was legal to sanction Bet Yisrael weddings. Although he was part of a board of rabbis who opposed him, he stood by his decision. He was the only rabbi in Israel who performed these rites. I used to bring couples from all over Israel to be married by him.

Chapter XXVI

There was a lull in the Ethiopian Jewish immigration. Shamir had promised to rescue more people, but nothing was happening. I called the prime minister's office and threatened to stage another demonstration. But Moshe Bar-Yuda, whom I trusted completely, told me to be patient; something was in the works. Apparently, a secret deal had been hatched between the Israeli government and the Sudanese. At last, two months after our demonstration, in 1984, "Operation Moses" was in full swing. Eight thousand Ethiopian Jews were airlifted to Israel.

Two Knesset members, Tamar Eshel and Yael Rome, proved to be most helpful in their resettlement and absorption. More people could have been rescued, but Dominitz, who previously had foiled our attempts, spilled the beans to the press. The other Arab nations were furious. The Sudanese leader lost his position. Finally, US President Reagan's Vice President Bush visited the refugee camps and gave the CIA orders to take out more people. They succeeded in saving another two thousand refugees. Yet there were some elderly and young members of Bet Yisrael left in the camps and other young activists – who had worked on behalf of Israel – were in prison and being tortured in Ethiopia.

At a press conference, the Israeli government declared that they had rescued all the Jews out of Ethiopia. "How can you say that?"

I shouted. "There are still another fifteen thousand of my people languishing in Ethiopia." This sparked a debate in the Knesset. Finally Yehuda Dominitz was obliged to resign and Chaim Aharoni took his place.

After all these efforts, I was exhausted. I had been working from my heart and soul, putting everything I had into the cause. It pained me to see others in it for their own aggrandizement or for political purposes. My Ethiopian confreres were divided into many different factions, which blinded them from seeing the whole picture. Though I tried to unite my community, too often the leaders were on ego trips and would not cooperate.

With whatever energy I had left, I gave it one more shot. In 1987, we staged a massive demonstration – about one thousand strong – in front of the Knesset and then smaller groups took over the vigil for a whole month. We demanded from Prime Minister Shamir that Israel save the rest of our brothers and sisters who were stranded in Ethiopia. There was also the matter of rescuing our imprisoned boys, whose "crime" was, as agents of Israel, they had tried to get some of Bet Yisrael out of Ethiopia via Djibouti and were caught in the process. But Israel refused to interfere. The government seemed to have dropped the whole matter. We tried to convince them that it was their responsibility to act. It seemed that the Israeli government didn't want to be drawn into the conflict.

So then we decided to approach this matter from a different perspective. We came up with the idea of staging a large concert to showcase the wonderful music and dances we had brought to Israel and at the same time to honor those who were instrumental in our rescue until then. We invited Prime Minister Shamir and others who had been involved, such as Irwin Cotler and Natan Sharansky (the outspoken Russian "prisoner of conscience"), to share our joy and happiness in living in Israel. Israeli musicians joined ours in the performance and, that evening, all four thousand people there experienced a togetherness they had never felt before. Shamir was pleasantly surprised. And in a separate room, one of our *kessim* recited a special blessing over him. Shamir smiled.

One reporter later remarked that it was the first time he saw our prime minister smile!

But the euphoria didn't last long. I continued to have more problems with my own people. I realized that they did not have the benefits I had, having been out in the world, where I had developed a broader perspective. Their vision was limited to the confines of their own communities. They lived by a kind of African tribalism; for example, when a position became vacant in the community, the job didn't necessarily go to the best man, but to someone in the group's hierarchy. I tried to get them to elect the right person for the job, but they didn't understand that kind of democracy. There was constant bickering. "United we stand, divided we fall" had no meaning for them. Today Israelis say, jokingly, that because the Ethiopians have so many different opinions, it's proof enough that they are authentic Jews!

In planning the concert, various groups wanted to have control over who was to speak at the concert and a few of the organizers craved the limelight for themselves. I asked that Yona Bogale, who was elderly now, be invited to address the assembly. Without the initial contact he had made between Ethiopia and Israel, we might never have achieved our exodus. I wanted very much to give him the honor of opening the festivities, but the committee – not knowing the history of our struggle – said no. They believed that God had brought them to the Promised Land, not individuals. They categorically refused my request.

Another incident happened which hurt me terribly. I had recommended that Moshe Bar-Yuda, an Israeli who had supported our endeavors for many years, speak at our celebration. Many years before, in 1958, as a young military officer, paratrooper, and an ordained rabbi, Moshe was called into the office of Ashkenazi Chief Rabbi Isaac Herzog, who sat him down and related to him all he knew about the Ethiopian Jews. Moshe was flabbergasted – he had never heard about us before. Rabbi Herzog announced that he had selected *him* to go to that jungle, because he was young and strong and had the moral attributes needed for the task ahead.

Moshe asked many questions, but didn't get all the answers, so he went to the Sephardi Rabbi Nissim for his opinion. He said: "What are you going to do with these black people?" Still in a quandary, Bar-Yuda left him and sought the advice of the rabbi who had ordained him, Professor Haim Gevaryahu. This scholar told him it would be a great *mitzvah* – fulfillment of a commandment – "to redeem the captives." Moshe made up his mind then and there to go.

That year (1958), some of the group who had come with me to Israel had decided to go back to Ethiopia before they had completed their education. Moshe Bar-Yuda escorted them home. He traveled to the remotest hills where Jewish communities were located. He even climbed the second highest mountain in Africa, Mount Semien, where he planted an Israeli flag. (Rothschild was celebrating his birthday there and met him on the mountain. They shook hands.) Moshe saw firsthand the conditions under which my people lived and foresaw that they would deteriorate. He stayed there for a whole year. When he returned to Israel, he spoke up against the government's unfair policy of neglect towards the Bet Yisrael. He made his case known in newspapers, on radio, and TV, at the expense of losing much of his prestige and some close friends.

In 1973 an edict was passed which forbade Israelis to speak about the issue, both inside and outside the country, or to encourage *aliyah* from Ethiopia. This did not stop Moshe. When I returned to Israel in 1976, I was taken aback when I heard him speak about the issue on TV. I recalled the time he had come to visit my school in Kfar Batya and immediately went out to meet with him. He, in turn, remembered me as a little boy. He encouraged me to continue my valuable work. Moshe Bar-Yuda was another one of the heroes I had wanted to honor at our festival, but was refused.

I had also wanted to give credit to other Israelis, Americans, and Canadians who had stuck their necks out for us, but I was stopped in my tracks. I felt it important to inform the new generation about how they got to where they were; they had to know the past in order to progress in a positive way into the future. But my peers didn't believe in altruism; they couldn't understand that people put themselves out and risked their lives and livelihood out of a moral commitment to them and to the Jewish people as a whole. They were convinced that I and the others did what we did for money or for some other selfish interests. To top it all off, they had no ability to share glory with others; they could only do that within their own families.

I became very disheartened. I had expected my people to work with me, to give me the energy to carry on, but instead they fought against me. Some were puppets of the government and followed their orders, with no questions asked. Yet I couldn't blame them; I knew that they didn't know better. It would probably take another generation or two for them to change their deep-seated attitudes.

I hadn't realized that all these confrontations had taken a toll on my health. An American friend, Dr. Doblen, came over to me after the concert and, looking very concerned, asked, "Baruch, what's happened to you? You've changed so much, you're so skinny. I think you're sick. Call me tomorrow." He gave me his number. He instructed me to go to his sister's house in Tel Aviv, where he arranged for her to take me to the hospital and to look after my needs. As I had no medical card, she kindly made all the arrangements and he, Dr. Doblen, paid all my bills. In the hospital, the doctors found that my sugar level was dangerously high and prescribed the appropriate medication. After a while my blood count was regulated, but relentless diabetes plagues me to this day.

The results of my efforts culminating in the huge concert ended with my physical collapse. One Israeli newspaper wrote: "Baruch finished the war! But today he is like a wounded animal. He taught the leaders how to fight for their rights; now they are spreading false rumors about him. The truth is that he did for his people what Begin had done for Israel."

The real truth of the matter was that I had found myself, as they say, "between a rock and a hard place." On one side, the Ethiopians claimed that I had become rich and had contacts with people in high places – they had seen a picture of me in the papers speaking to a senator. On the other side, the Israelis alleged that I was anti-Israeli, that I had gone all around the world saying bad things about them.

In spite of the malicious gossip about me, I tried to figure out some way that the Israeli government could rescue the imprisoned men. I came up with an idea and met with Haim Halachmi and two Mossad men to discuss it. I told them that when I was in school in Israel, I had befriended an Ethiopian Christian boy, Kassa Kebede, whose father was an officer in Emperor Haile Selassie's government before the revolution, and had sent him there "to get a good education." We remained good friends and I offered to talk to him. I knew that he was also on good terms with Menghistu Haile Mariam, the (totalitarian) head of state of Ethiopia (1979–91), who became the civilian president of the renamed People's Democratic Republic of Ethiopia in 1987. They advised me to go ahead and talk to him.

Kassa was then the Ethiopian representative to the Food and Agricultural Organization of the UN, but when I got to Geneva, he was out of town. Instead, I met with his wife, who then relayed the whole story to him. Before long, Kassa contacted me and told me that he knew some of the men who were in jail and felt very sad about what had happened to them. He claimed that had he known earlier, he might have been able to do something, but once they were in prison it was very difficult to change things. Nevertheless, he promised to try his best. Later, when he came to Israel, we met twice and he agreed to participate in the whole rescue operation on behalf of the Ethiopian government.

Prime Minister Shamir, meanwhile, went to the Union of African Countries and brought up the subject of the prisoners and the need to rescue the rest of Bet Yisrael, who were still suffering in Ethiopia.* He then invited Senator Rudy Boschwitz and Congressman Gary Ackerman to meet with him in Israel, where they devised a plan to discuss the issues with representatives of the Ethiopian government. Kassa was one of the negotiators for Ethiopia

---

* See appendix 3.

and gave our side a hard time at first, but then became cooperative. Finally, Menghistu agreed to allow the Jews to leave on Ethiopian or Israeli planes in return for thirty-five million dollars, to cover the cost of releasing the prisoners and for airlifting the remaining fifteen thousand people to Israel. A member of the Israeli Defense Ministry went to Ethiopia to make sure the money stayed in the bank there until it was needed.

In April, small planeloads of people began to leave Addis Ababa every week, and then the process accelerated until May 24 and 25, 1991, when "Operation Solomon" went into full gear. In two days, 14,310 Ethiopians were delivered from oppression to the yearned-for Holy Land. Its success is thanks largely to the backing of President George Bush, the determined involvement of US Senator Boschwitz and Congressman Ackerman; the USA's United Israel Appeal and the Jewish Agency who, together, funded the venture; and to the dedicated Israeli airmen, servicemen, frogmen, etc., who carried through the whole procedure without a hitch. There was such jubilation! This was the fulfillment of a messianic dream. Kassa himself flew with the last group to Israel. I met him in Jerusalem and we had a great time reminiscing about our youth.

With the completion of "Operation Solomon" in 1991, we had rescued a total of about thirty-seven thousand Ethiopian Jews. There was only a handful of Bet Yisrael members left in Ethiopia, mostly elderly people who didn't want to leave their homes at this stage of their lives. I breathed a sigh of relief and gratitude knowing that all our efforts – mine and those of our friends in the United States, Canada, and Israel – were not in vain.

Chapter XXVII

I returned to Canada in 1993, as my daughter, Yaffa, was going to have her bat mitzvah. During that time, my organization in Israel staged a demonstration against what was then known as "the blood scandal." My people had learned that blood donated by Bet Yisrael was not being used for medical purposes. It was suspected of being tainted with AIDS and was destroyed, thrown in the garbage instead of being used to save lives as the donors had of course intended. Our pride was sorely hurt. When the mounted police came to disrupt the protest, some of the demonstrators threw pepper in the horses' eyes. Finally, the authorities agreed to accept our blood as equal to the others.

After the bat mitzvah, I went back to Israel because I wanted to be with my family, especially my father, Zeleke Demoze, who had made *aliyah* in 1991. I had a strong desire to be close to him and to get to know him better. Even though I was then nearly fifty years old, I felt almost like a baby; I had no support from my community and suffered from abandonment. Father was a big strapping man, a stalwart Jew, who was very proud of my achievements. He told me that wherever he went, people admired him because he was "Baruch's father." I wallowed in the comfort of his warmth and love.

My father had learned Italian as a child and was able to read

English. Prayer was very important to him; he didn't care what synagogue he went to, as long as he was with other Jews. He had a certain charisma and prestige which commanded respect. He was a well-known poet, who had received accolades for his works and was revered by the Ethiopians. When he was in Israel, a number of his poems were translated into Hebrew and were printed in the newspapers to wide acclaim. He had written one poem about me – how he missed me when I was small – that was very deep and sensitive; it makes me cry every time I read it. My favorite poem of them all describes his own beleaguered life. It is an allegory about a dog named *Michal*, which means "patience." Without Michal, he wrote, he couldn't have survived.

Father and his wife came to Israel when he was in his eighties (his children had come before). He was so thrilled to be there that he naively was determined to join the army to defend the Holy Land. But, of course, he was much too old. Unfortunately he became paralyzed six years later. His youngest son took care of him for the next six years. Father died in 2002, in his nineties.

Yaffa, age thirteen, in Israel

Chapter XXVIII

My people – especially the children – were gradually becoming assimilated into the mainstream of Israeli society. This was very gratifying to me, except that I feared that our particular kind of rich Jewish culture was getting lost in the process. I decided to form an organization to preserve our cultural heritage. I approached the mayor of Rehovot, who generously allotted us a lovely piece of land near the Weitzman Institute, to build a cultural center. With the help of some friends from the USA and Toronto, we set about designing a beautiful architectural site for the "Culture and Heritage Center of the Jews of Ethiopia." Our plan includes a theater with tiers of benches in the open air designed to seat eight hundred people, a small replica of a Bet Yisrael village with a river running through it, gardens with native herbs for medicinal purposes, and a memorial to the four thousand people who died in Sudan. With support from the Americans, Canadians, and many Israelis, we held a ceremony to launch the project and joyously laid the cornerstone.

That very day, I received a court order from the Balahachin Organization – an Ethiopian Jewish organization supported by the Israeli government – to stop proceedings at once. The Bahalachin claimed to be the true representatives of Bet Yisrael and the only ones entitled to create the center. I had previously invited them to participate in the planning, but they firmly refused. Even Meir Tzabban, the minister of absorption, had tried to bring us together, but didn't succeed either. The legal battles went on for two years until we finally won our case. In the meantime, we were unable to campaign for support and our funds dried up.

During that time, the distinguished lawyer and professor Ed Morgan of the Canadian Jewish Congress visited Israel with a group of people and was fascinated by our project. He and his wife offered to help. He suggested that if I came to Canada again, I should meet with him and some of his friends and they might be able to do something for us.

I did come to Canada in 2002 on a fund-raising tour for the center. But sadly, when I got there, I became very ill and had to go on dialysis three times a week. I had planned to visit Ed Morgan in Toronto to speak to him and a group of other interested men and women, but, unfortunately, I couldn't make it. The project is now in limbo. My fervent hope today is to recover as soon as possible – with the help of a kidney transplant – and to restart my activities to speed up the building of the cultural and heritage center. I dream of going back to my beloved Israel and of reuniting with my family and my people.

Addendum by Phyllis Pinchuk

*I*n November 2004, while in Israel, my husband and I, along
with our Canadian friend Taras Gabora (a well-known violin
teacher), were invited by Rabbi Moshe Bar-Yuda to attend a
recording session of the chants performed by the Bet Yisrael kessim
(priests). The rabbi, who is also a musicologist, was determined to
record their music for posterity. (When he had asked them to come
to the studio to record their songs, they protested, saying, "We don't
sing, we pray!") An interpreter introduced us to these five impressive
men, four of whom were wearing their distinguished white robes and
headgear. When they heard that we were friends of Baruch Tegegne,
they were overwhelmed! They claimed that, if not for Baruch, they
would not be alive today. So much was their gratitude that they had
tears in their eyes when they spoke of him. I suggested to Moshe that
he ask the kessim to offer a prayer for Baruch's health. No sooner
did he pose the question than they all, as one man, began to chant a
prayer for his complete recovery. Moshe had the technician make a
CD of the prayer, which we delivered to Baruch just one week later
upon our return to Montreal.

In August 2005, Baruch Tegegne had a kidney transplant at the
Royal Victoria Hospital in Montreal and at the time of this writing
is doing quite well.

Acknowledgments

Thank you to my supportive husband, Abe Pinchuk, and our children and their spouses, David and Paulette Pinchuk, Len and Diane Pinchuk, Josh and Cindy Pinchuk, and Amy Pinchuk and Mark Meland. To friends Sylvia Stipelman, Taras Gabora, Sheba Meland, Moshe Bar-Yuda, Yudit Rotem, the Roses, and the Kalichmans, for their interest and encouragement. To the Montreal Jewish Library, for their research assistance. To consultants Dr. Ephraim Isaac, John Metcalf, and Professor Howard Lenhoff for their unstinting help. To Dr. Norman Doidge for his indirect assistance. And to the Jewish Community Foundation of Montreal, for helping to realize the publication of this project.

                                         – Phyllis Pinchuk

I am deeply grateful to all my friends mentioned in the book, as well as to Scott Rosenberg, The Lester and Edna Shapiro Family Foundation, Harlan Jacobs, Yvonne Margo, Abe Pinchuk, Nira Friedman and Dr. Lawrence Kleiman, and Rabbi Ronnie and Mrs. Karen Cahana for all they have done for me. I am very appreciative of Simcha Jacobovici's drive to get me a kidney transplant and I will forever be indebted to the donor and the marvelous team of doctors and nurses who gave me back my life. Last, but not least, I wish to thank Phyllis Pinchuk from the bottom of my heart for her patience, empathy, and understanding in putting down on paper my life story.

                                         – Baruch Tegegne

Kessim recording chants, Tel Aviv, 2004

Appendix 1

BARUCH'S LONG JOURNEY TO ISRAEL

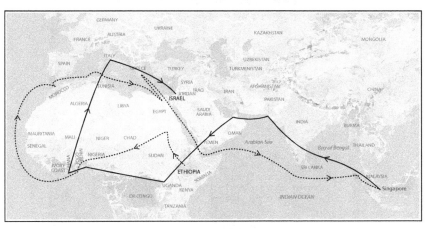

············· From Ethiopia, by land to Nigeria and by sea to Singapore
——————— Then by plane from Singapore back to Nigeria, to Rome and finally to Israel

1000 mi
2000 km

Appendix 2

The B'nai B'rith Hillel Foundation

at Brandeis University

proudly bestows

The Ninth Annual SHIFRA AND PUAH Memorial Award

upon

YURI BEN GAD

and

BARUCH TEGEGNE

this April 24, 1985 ~ 4 Iyyar, 5745

Shifra and Puah, the courageous Biblical midwives, engaged in a supreme act of civil disobedience. On pain of execution, they defied Pharoh's decree to kill all newborn Hebrew males. Their heroism earned them a place of distinction in the Bible and in the history of the Jewish people.

Yuri Ben Gad *and* **Baruch Tegegne**, *leaders of the Beta Yisrael, have devoted their lives to the freedom of their brethren, both while in Ethiopia and in their current home of Israel. Courageously, they made return visits to their native land to teach and assist those Jews who were unable to escape. Today they serve as leaders in the absorption process of Ethiopians who have been brought to Israel.*

(Rabbi) Albert S. Axelrad	Hillel Director and Chaplain
Ora Gladstone	Assistant Director
Naomi Bar-Yam	Program Director
Michael Miller	Advisory Council Chair

206

Appendix 3

Tuesday, July 28, 1987 Th

PM asks OAU to help Ethiopian Jews

By ANDY COURT

Prime Minister Shamir called last night upon African leaders now meeting in Addis Ababa to press for the release of Jews remaining in Ethiopia.

"These Jews want only one thing," Shamir said. "Let them leave Ethiopia and come to Israel."

The prime minister spoke at an assembly of 1,000 Ethiopian Jews and their supporters in Jerusalem. Beiteynu, BA, set up to highlight the plight of Ethiopian families seeking reunification.

No one knows exactly how many Jews remain in Ethiopia, but a middle-range estimate is 15,000. At least 1,000 children now in Israel have parents who are still in Ethiopia and are unable to leave.

Human rights lawyer Irwin Cotler, who represented former Prisoner of Zion Natan Sharansky and now represents black South African leader Nelson Mandela, read an appeal that 15 Nobel Laureates have sent to Ethiopian leader Mengistu Haile Mariam on behalf of Ethiopian Jewry. The Nobel leaders called upon union leaders throughout the world to aid the Ethiopian cause.

Sharansky drew parallels between the problems of Soviet and Ethiopian Jewry. He also criticized the Israeli government for not putting enough emphasis on immigration. "The criterion of the success of

every government is the rate of aliya," Sharansky said, sometimes he said he has the impression that the government doesn't realize that.

Sharansky added that one thing that encouraged him while he was in

One of the hundreds of Ethiopians who gathered at Binyenei Ha'uma in Jerusalem yesterday receives a warm handshake from Prime Minister Shamir. (Y. Zion/Melki)

prison in the USSR was reading in a Soviet propaganda organ that "Jewish agents" had brought the Ethiopians to Israel.

Church Geveve adds:

Immigration and Absorption Minister Ya'acov Tsur urged Ethiopian-Jewish youth in Israel to be strong and said that despite their pain at the separation from their families, they must integrate themselves as much as possible and help members of their community.

Tsur was replying to the Knesset plenum to motions for the agenda on the plight of Ethiopian Jewry by Mapam MK Chaika Grossman and the Likud's Miriam Ta'asa-Glaser.

Tsur praised the quiet dignity of the Ethiopian immigrants. Their appeal for family reunification, he said was shared by everyone except that must also be handed to the Jews remaining in Ethiopia to Israel.

Speaker Shlomo Hillel, in an unusual move, made his own appeal to the representatives of the community waited in the distinguished visitors gallery.

Referring to the assembly that he was later to chair at Binyenei Ha'uma, Hillel assured the community they had the country's understanding of their entire cause.

It was wherethings looked darkest, said Hillel, that help was most at hand, as had already been proven

Index

About the Authors

Baruch Tegegne was born in 1944 in Wozaba, Ethiopia, a remote Jewish hillside village. He has worked his entire life to help bring his people to the Land of Israel, which they cherished from afar for two thousand years. Today he lives in Montreal, Canada, but is determined to go back to Israel to be with his people and continue building the Cultural and Heritage Center of the Jews of Ethiopia in Rehovot.

Phyllis Schwartzman Pinchuk was born in Montreal, Canada, in 1929. She attended the Talmud Torah, one of the first Hebrew day schools in Montreal, and graduated from the Montreal Hebrew Teacher's Seminary. She was a co-founder of Limud Publications, a volunteer nonprofit organization that produced teaching tools for heritage programs, Jewish holidays, history and values. She also served for a few years as Supplementary Education consultant for the Jewish Educational Council of Montreal.

Phyllis was introduced to Baruch Tegegne at a book club meeting where he spoke of his harrowing struggles in his effort to rescue his people. Her comment that he must put his saga down in writing led to their collaboration.